IN HIS PRESENCE
Dr. Tommy Combs

LIVING
WORD
BOOKS

IN HIS PRESENCE

Copyright © 2019 by Dr. Tommy Combs
EMAIL: tommy.livingwordbooks@gmail.com
WEBSITE: www.evangelisttommycombs.org

ISBN: 978-1-7336334-0-6

Published by:

LIVING
WORD
B▨▨KS

PO Box 1000, Dora, Alabama 35062

Layout and design by: Mercy Hope

Dedication:

To the Father, Son and Holy Ghost.
In your presence is fullness of joy (Psalm 16:11).
That is all that really matters, in this life
and in the life to come.

Acknowledgement:

As with all of my other books, the book you now
hold in your hands began on the desk of my publisher,
Neil Eskelin. Unfortunately, Neil did not get to see this book
come to completion, as he passed away in August of 2018.

His promotion to Heaven means a
new season for my book ministry.

I could not finish this book without honoring
the man whose skill for writing and publishing
were only overshadowed by his friendship.

I now have a new book production team and my own
publishing division of my ministry, but I will always
remember Neil Eskelin for being the friend and publisher
who made it possible for Living Word Ministries
to begin reaching thousands through my books.

—Dr. Tommy Combs

CONTENTS

Introduction

God's Presence and Power on:

INTRODUCTION

There is no touch like God's touch.

Over the years, I have had the privilege of personally meeting and sitting under the ministry of dedicated men and women who preached and prayed with a special anointing from Heaven. I could discern in my spirit when God's power was present and when it was not.

This caused me to wonder: How did the Lord speak to the prophets and great men and women of God in the Old Testament? And what led to such mighty miracles among the apostles and preachers in the New Testament—not just through Jesus, but in the lives of ordinary people just like you and me?

On these pages you are going to meet Abraham, Isaac, and Jacob. You will also meet women such as Deborah, Esther, and Mary. You will learn how God touched them—and how, in return, they touched God.

You will also discover how the same anointing that fell on the prophets of old descended on men and women such as the noted British Evangelist Smith Wigglesworth and Kathryn Kuhlman.

HOWEVER, THIS BOOK IS NOT JUST ABOUT THEM —IT'S ABOUT YOU!

My sincere prayer is that the contents of this book will unlock the door to blessing and give you access to the throne of God. I pray you will receive a fresh, life-changing touch of His power … *In His Presence.*

—DR. TOMMY COMBS

chapter 1

God's Presence and Power on
NOAH

As we begin this journey, I am reminded of one of the first Bible characters I was ever introduced to. His name was Noah. As children in Sunday School we listened spellbound to the stories of the animals going into this huge boat that Noah built.

What I didn't know at the time, is that after the fall of mankind, Noah was the first man documented in Scripture to experience the amazing power and presence of God.

As men and women began to multiply after the miracle of creation, the Almighty looked down and was saddened and horrified at the wickedness and evil that ran rampant throughout the land. So much so that *the Lord was sorry that He had made man on the earth and was grieved in His heart. So the Lord said, 'I will destroy man whom I have created from the face of the earth'* (Genesis 6:7).

God would do this by causing a devastating flood. But He would save a remnant by choosing a man to build an ark so that at least one family and two of every living creature would survive.

In scouring the earth, the Creator found an individual who was so righteous that Scripture calls him *"perfect in his generations"* (verse 9). His name was Noah.

IT IS IN THIS STORY
THAT A DIVINE FORCE
IS INTRODUCED
FOR THE FIRST TIME.
THE WORD IS "GRACE."

The Bible tell us *"Noah found grace in the eyes of the Lord"* (Genesis 6:8).

God's gift of grace is strong enough to defeat wickedness and evil. We know this is true because *"Where sin abounded, grace abounded much more"* (Romans 5:20).

Noah also received an anointing of physical power. How else could one man find the strength and perseverance needed to build a massive ark?

While everyone ridiculed him because they hadn't seen rain for years, Noah followed God's command. I am sure you know the rest of the story.

What moved this righteous man was the fact that *"By faith Noah, being divinely warned of things not yet seen, moved with godly fear"* (Hebrews 11:7).

In other words, the Lord gave Noah a glimpse of the future, and it placed a passion within him to stay focused on the task at hand.

A Special Anointing

When the rain ended, and the ark rested on top of Mount Ararat, God introduced another powerful force—the Holy Spirit.

As the waters began to recede, Noah sent out a dove, and *"the dove came to him in the evening, and behold a freshly plucked olive leaf was in her mouth"* (Genesis 8:11).

That same Spirit, while gentle, is also mighty. When John baptized Jesus in the Jordan River, *"Jesus came up immediately from the water; and behold, the heavens were opened to Him, and He saw the Spirit of God descending like a dove and alighting upon Him"* (Matthew 3:16).

Jesus knew the dove was only a visual symbol of something far more amazing. He declared, *"You shall receive power when that Holy Spirit has come upon you"* (Acts 1:8). We see this on the Day of Pentecost when *"there came a sound from heaven, as of a rushing mighty wind ... and they were all filled with the Holy Spirit and began to speak with other tongues as the Spirit gave them utterance"* (Acts 2:2, 4).

After the great flood, God made a covenant with Noah that He would never destroy the earth again in the same way.

> IT IS MY PRAYER THAT
> THE ANOINTING WHICH
> FELL ON NOAH,
> AND FOREVER
> CHANGED HIS LIFE,
> WILL REST ON YOU.

This anointing will give you grace ... and so much more. It will awaken within you a passion to preach righteousness, equip you with the strength to accomplish God's purpose, and fill you with the power of the Holy Spirit.

chapter 2

God's Presence and Power on
ABRAHAM

We often use the term, "Father Abraham" because God promised that this patriarch of old would become *"a father of many nations"* (Genesis 17:4)—and he did!

Here was a 75-year-old man whom the Lord told to leave his country and travel to a land he did not know. God made this vow: *"I will bless you and make your name great; and you shall be a blessing. I will bless those who bless you, and I will curse him who curses you; and in you all the families of the earth shall be blessed"* (Genesis 12:2-3).

The reason Abraham was able to accomplish

incredible things for God is because, as the Apostle Paul writes, *"He did not waver at the promise of God through unbelief, but was strengthened in faith, giving glory to God"* (Romans 4:20).

HE NOT ONLY BELIEVED, BUT BECAUSE OF HIS UNSHAKABLE FAITH, HE RECEIVED POWER AND STRENGTH.

Abraham, without a shadow of doubt, knew the source of his blessing. That's why when he arrived in Canaan, the first thing he did at Shechem was to *"[build] an altar to the Lord, who had appeared to him"* (Genesis 12:7).

The power from above rested on Abraham. At one point, God told him to look north, south, east, and west … *"for all the land which you see I give to you and your descendants forever"* (Genesis 13:15). It was the territory Israel claims for its own today.

THE PROMISE

God's continual presence gave Abraham faith and sustained him through the toughest of times. Every sacrifice was well worth it.

When the Almighty delivered the covenant, He also gave him a sign from Heaven to confirm His word. It was the promise of a child, which sounded improbable since Abraham and Sarah were way past their childbearing years. The combination of their longevity and her infertility made the thought of having children seem impossible.

You can imagine Sarah's disbelief when this promise was revealed to her. In fact, she laughed and questioned, *"Shall I surely bear a child, since I am old?"* (Genesis 18:13).

Yes, Sarah did become pregnant and gave birth to a son, Isaac. God did fulfill His promise.

Regarding Sarah becoming a mother in her old age, God asked her a question that has resonated through the ages, *"Is anything too hard for the Lord?"* (verse 13).

I can tell you from personal experience that there is no problem too difficult for God to solve, no river that is uncrossable, and no mountain He can't tunnel through. In my ministry, I have witnessed the Lord performing miracles of healing and deliverance and I have seen countless lives restored. What He did for Abraham and Sarah, He is still doing today for those who dare to believe in Him.

THE BLESSING IS FOR YOU!

Let me share some good news. If you have accepted Jesus Christ as your Savior, you have been promised the divine covenant inheritance that belonged to Abraham. As Paul wrote to the believers at Galatia, *"For you are all sons of God through faith in Christ Jesus. For as many of you as were baptized into Christ have put on Christ. There is neither Jew nor Greek, there is neither slave nor free, there is neither male nor female; for you are all one in Christ Jesus. And if you are Christ's, then you are Abraham's seed, and heirs according to the promise"* (Galatians 3:26-29).

The impact of this is enormous.

AS THE "SEED" OF
FATHER ABRAHAM,
YOU ARE BOTH THE RECIPIENT
OF THE GREAT BLESSING
AND THE INSTRUMENT
THROUGH WHICH
THE BLESSING AND FAVOR
OF GOD IS PASSED ON
TO OTHERS.

You are a child of the covenant!

chapter 3

God's Presence and Power on
ISAAC

We are first introduced to Isaac when he was a baby—the long-promised son and heir of Abraham and Sarah. As the Lord told him, *"Sarah your wife shall bear a son, and you shall call him Isaac; and I will establish my covenant with him as an everlasting covenant, and with his descendants after him"* (Genesis 17:19). What God began with Abraham was going to continue through his beloved son.

It's amazing how the anointing of the Lord rested on Isaac. Scripture tells us that fourteen years earlier, Abraham had fathered another child—Ishmael—through Hagar, his wife's hand-maiden in a defiant act of impatience and disobedience. When Isaac was about two years old, a feast was being held to celebrate the young lad being weaned from his mother Sarah. It was at these festivities when some extremely rude behavior on the part of Ishmael resulted in Hagar and her son being evicted from the household. From that point on, Isaac had no competitor for his father's favor and attention.

One of the most powerful lessons in Scripture took place when God commanded Abraham to take Isaac to Mount Moriah and offer his beloved son as a sacrifice.

What he was being asked to do was almost unthinkable, but Abraham obeyed God. The next morning, Abraham saddled up his donkeys and brought along some wood for the burnt offering as he headed for the mountain.

Three days later, Abraham built the altar, tied the limbs of Isaac together, and laid him on the wood. In a solitary act of total faith, Abraham called on all the courage he could find as he lifted his knife high above Isaac. In a faith-defining moment, before he could plunge the knife into his son, something incredible happened. An angel cried out for him to stop, saying, *"Do not lay your hand on the lad, or do anything to him; for now I know that you fear God, since you have not withheld your son, your only son, from Me"* (Genesis 22:12). Instead, the angel told him to take a ram from the nearby thicket for the sacrifice, and Isaac's life was spared.

There is only one conclusion we can draw from his story:

TOTAL OBEDIENCE
AND DEVOTION
MOVES THE HEART
AND HAND OF GOD,
THEREBY BRINGING LIFE
INTO IMPOSSIBLE SITUATIONS!

Sowing in a Famine

The Lord's ongoing blessing on Isaac's life is undeniable. When he was older, there came a severe famine that would cause any farmer to be disheartened and perhaps give up. But not Isaac. God told him, *"Do not go down to Egypt; live in the land of which I shall tell you"* (Genesis 26:2).

The Bible records, *"Then Isaac sowed in that land, and reaped in the same year a hundredfold; and the Lord blessed him"* (verse 12). He became the prosperous owner of countless flocks, herds, and servants.

God's hand remained on Isaac and his wife, Rebekah. Isaac was 60 years old when Rebekah gave birth to twin boys, Jacob and Esau.

What a lesson for you and me. We may think we have all the answers and are capable of making our own decisions. All too often, men and women attempt to chart their own course, leaving God out of their lives altogether.

Isaac was fully aware that he was under the covenant of his father, and when the Lord spoke, he listened.

In the natural, it would have been foolish to plant crops during a drought. But what's foolish to man can become a feast to God. The foolish man ignores God while the wise man follows His voice even when it does not appear to make sense.

There are many reasons the presence of the Lord rested on Isaac. First, he was submissive (he didn't protest when he was laid on the sacrificial altar). Second, he was a man of prayer. At Beersheba, *he built an altar ... and called on the name of the Lord"* (Genesis 26:25). Third, he was a man of peace. When the herdsmen bickered over where he was digging a well, he didn't argue but just moved to another site (Genesis 26:20-33). Most significant, he was a man of firm faith. Like his father before him, he believed God—and the blessings followed! When he got In His Presence.

ISAAC'S WILLINGNESS
TO LISTEN AND OBEY
WAS CENTRAL TO
HIS LIFE OF FAITH.

ALLOW HIS EXAMPLE
TO INFUSE YOUR HEART
WITH A DEEPER DESIRE
TO FOLLOW GOD'S VOICE
AT ANY COST.

chapter 4

God's Presence and Power on JACOB

When twins are born, one always arrives first! In the case of Esau and Jacob, Esau entered the world first so he was the oldest—this meant he was in line to receive the birthright of his father, Isaac.

Well, it didn't quite work out that way. Once, when Jacob was cooking some stew, Esau came home from tending the flock, smelled the aroma and demanded, *"Give me some of that."*

Jacob was quick on the trigger and responded, *"Sell me your birthright and I'll give you what you ask"*—which, foolishly, Esau did.

Later, through trickery and deception, Jacob convinced his blind and ailing father, Isaac, to give him the blessing a father traditionally bestows on the first born son.

When Esau discovered he had been deceived, he vowed to kill his brother. Sensing that his life was in mortal danger, Jacob fled to take refuge in a place called Haran with his uncle, Laban.

On the journey, Jacob had an encounter with God that changed his life forever. When the sun set, he placed his weary head on a rock and went to sleep. In the night he had a dream in which *"a ladder was set up on the earth, and its top reached to heaven; and there the angels of God were ascending and descending on it"* (Genesis 28:12). It's called "Jacob's Ladder."

Above the ladder, the Lord was standing and spoke these words: *"I am the Lord God of Abraham your father and the God of Isaac; the land on which you lie I will give to you and your descendants"* (verse 13).

The next morning, Jacob woke from his sleep and exclaimed, *"Surely the Lord is in this place, and I did not know it"* (verse 16). With fear and trembling, he said, *"How awesome is this place! This is none other than the house of God, and this is the gate of heaven!"* (verse 17).

A Second Encounter

In Haran, Jacob fell in love with Laban's daughter Rachel. Desiring her hand in marriage, he had to work the land for many years of servitude before the two were allowed to become man and wife. After they were married, Laban still wouldn't release Jacob from the work, so one evening Jacob and his family slipped away and headed back to the land of his father.

This is when the second major encounter with God occurred.

One night, while Jacob was asleep, Scripture details how *"a Man wrestled with him until the breaking of day"* (Genesis 32:24). But when the

"Man"—God in the likeness of man—saw that He couldn't prevail against him, He touched the socket of Jacob's hip, which came out of joint.

The Man said, "Let Me go, because the sun is coming up."

Jacob answered, *"I will not let You go unless You bless me!"*

So, He said to him, *"What is your name?"*

"Jacob," he replied.

And He responded, *"Your name shall no longer be called Jacob, but Israel; for you have struggled with God and with men, and have prevailed"* (verse 28). So Jacob called the place Peniel: *"For I have seen God face to face, and my life is preserved"* (verse 30).

The most compelling part of the story is that, when Jacob was nearing home, he looked down the road and saw his brother, Esau, coming toward him with four hundred men.

What would happen? Would Esau now try

to take his revenge and kill Jacob? Just the opposite took place. What a scene it was when *"Esau ran to meet him, and embraced him, and fell on his neck and kissed him, and they wept"* (Genesis 33:4).

THERE IS NOTHING TO COMPARE WITH A PERSONAL ENCOUNTER WITH GOD.

In this case, it was so powerful that the name of one man forever became the name of a nation: *Israel.*

Jacob's life is full of experiences that many individuals can relate to. He attempted to steal from his own brother, then the father of the woman he loved took advantage of him.

Ultimately, his story gives us a powerful picture of reconciliation and restoration, reminding us that this is the life we are called to as sons and daughters of God.

chapter 5

God's Presence and Power on
JOSEPH

It wasn't pleasant being Jacob's favorite son, but this was true of Joseph—and it landed him in a heap of trouble. In fact, his brothers hated him.

Joseph was a dreamer. He made the catastrophic mistake of telling his brothers one of his significant dreams: *"There we were, binding sheaves in the field. Then behold, my sheaf arose and also stood upright; and indeed your sheaves stood all around and bowed down to my sheaf"* (Genesis 37:7).

His brothers got the message and inquired, "Does that mean you are going to reign over us?" As a result, they despised him even more.

The jealousy became so heated that one day, when Joseph went out into the field to see his older brothers, they saw him in the distance and said, *"Look, this dreamer is coming!"* (verse 19).

Immediately, they conspired to kill him by throwing him in a pit and telling their father, Jacob, that some wild animals had torn his body apart. But not wanting to actually shed his blood, when a camel caravan came by headed for Egypt, they pulled him out of the pit and sold him to the merchants. Then they went home with Joseph's coat of many colors. The brothers had soaked the garment in the blood of a goat as evidence which would support the false story they had concocted of how their brother had been killed by animals.

This was the beginning of one of the most dramatic accounts in Scripture—and how the almighty hand of God can reach down and lift us out of any situation to accomplish His will and purpose.

Joseph landed in Egypt and was immediately sold to Potiphar, an officer of Pharaoh and captain of the guard.

Potiphar was so impressed with Joseph that he entrusted him with more and more responsibility. But a lie by the officer's wife (that Joseph tried to seduce her) landed Joseph in prison.

As it happened, Pharaoh had a dream that couldn't be interpreted by the seers of the day. God entrusted Joseph with the answer. As a result, the king called him, *"a man in whom is the Spirit of God"* (Genesis 41:38).

THE PRESENCE OF THE LORD WAS SO EVIDENT ON JOSEPH THAT PHARAOH MADE HIM GOVERNOR OVER ALL OF EGYPT.

When a major drought scorched the earth, Joseph was placed in charge of storing and distributing all of the grain in the land. There was also a severe food shortage in Israel. It was so serious that Jacob sent several of his sons to Egypt to buy grain. Of course, the request of their father would require them to appeal to the governor in charge of the supplies … face to face.

They found themselves bowing unknowingly before Joseph, their brother, exactly as the young man had dreamed many years earlier. Their request was granted and they returned home loaded with food.

God Meant It for Good

On a subsequent visit, Joseph dramatically revealed himself to his brothers, *"Please come near to me,"* he ordered. As they did, he told them, *"I am Joseph your brother, whom you sold into Egypt"* (Genesis 45:4).

As you can imagine, the brothers were shocked; they were greatly dismayed in his presence. But Joseph assured them, *"Do not … be grieved or angry with yourselves because you sold me here; for God sent me before you to preserve life"* (verse 5).

It was a time of weeping and rejoicing. Joseph learned that his father was still alive, and soon the entire family moved to Egypt and settled in the land of Goshen.

THE TWELVE SONS BECAME THE TWELVE TRIBES OF ISRAEL.

When Jacob passed from this life, the brothers gathered around Joseph and once more begged for forgiveness. Falling to their faces they cried, "Behold, we are your servants" (Genesis 50:18).

Joseph reassured them, *"Do not be afraid, for am I in the place of God? But as for you, you meant evil against me; but God meant it for good, in order to bring it about as it is this day, to save many people alive"* (Genesis 50:19-20).

Joseph's life is a powerful reminder that the Lord calls his sons and daughters to walk in love and forgiveness. Those who take up this call are uniquely positioned to reveal the heart of the Father to the world.

chapter 6

God's Presence *and* Power *on*
MOSES

There is no substitute for a personal, intimate relationship with God. This is what gave Moses his incredible ability to lead the children of Israel.

According to Scripture, *"There has not arisen in Israel a prophet like Moses, who knew the Lord face to face"* (Deuteronomy 34:10).

If you think you are too old to do great exploits for God, think again! Moses was in his eightieth year when the Lord called him into a "deliverance ministry" unlike anything the world had ever known. He spent the next 40 years on a divine adventure.

It all began when Moses was tending sheep for his father-in-law, Jethro, on the back side of the desert. As he came to Mount Horeb, an angel of the Lord appeared to him in a flame of fire from the middle of a bush—incredibly, the bush was not consumed.

God called out to him from the fire, saying, *"Moses, Moses!"*

He answered, *"Here I am"* (Exodus 3:4).

That's when the Lord told Moses of the plight of the children of Israel, and that he had been chosen to lead God's people out of Egyptian bondage.

Moses, feeling inadequate, questioned, *"Who am I that I should go to Pharaoh, and that I should bring the children of Israel out of Egypt?"* (verse 11).

THE "I AM"

God assured Moses that He would work miracles and give him the authority to accomplish this challenging task. But even then, Moses was hesitant. At one point he argued, *"O my Lord, I am not eloquent … I am slow of speech and slow of tongue"* (Exodus 4:10).

The "I AM" answered, *"Who has made man's mouth? Or who makes the mute, the deaf, the seeing, or the blind? Have not I, the Lord? Now therefore, go, and I will be with your mouth and teach you what you shall say"* (verses 11-12).

WHAT AN ADVENTURE IT WAS! UNDER THE ANOINTING AND POWER OF GOD, MOSES TOLD PHARAOH, *"LET MY PEOPLE GO!"*

It took a series of plagues before Pharaoh relented and the historic exodus began. The children of Israel were headed for the Promised Land.

On the wilderness journey, Moses was constantly surrounded by a sea of negativity, but he rose above the murmurings and discontent, remaining faithful to God's commission and command. This is a powerful challenge that still resonates today in a world filled with negativity and darkness.

On the Mountain

Moses's personal encounters with the Great Jehovah were earthshaking. When their leader, Moses, went to the top of Mount Sinai to talk with God, the people could not personally see themselves doing the same. They told him, *"You speak with us, and we will hear; but let not God speak with us, lest we die"* (Exodus 20:19). This same fear of a higher power is expressed by many today. They seem frightened to be in His holy presence and have a close relationship with Him.

It is incredible what happened as Moses stepped out in faith and entered into the anointing. As a result, the Red Sea parted, water flowed out of a rock, and manna rained down from heaven!

I MARVEL AT HOW
MOSES ACCOMPLISHED
THE IMPOSSIBLE
THROUGH THE LORD'S
MIGHTY POWER.

IT LITERALLY CHANGED
THE ENTIRE COURSE
OF JEWISH HISTORY.

There are two major lessons we need to learn from the life of the prophet Moses. First, you are never too old to respond to God's voice. Second, if your heavenly Father calls you to a monumental task, He will supply you with the supernatural power necessary to see it accomplished.

Hallelujah!

chapter 7

God's Presence *and* Power *on* JOSHUA

From the beginning of the Exodus, a man by the name of Joshua remained close to Moses. Once a former slave in Egypt, Joshua became Moses's military commander when the Israelites defeated the Amalekites at Rephidim.

The two were so linked together that Joshua accompanied Moses at least halfway up the mountain when the tablets of stone containing the Ten Commandments were given (Exodus 24:13-14).

When it was time to scout out the Promised Land, Joshua was one of the twelve men who were commissioned to go—and one of only two men who came back with a positive, encouraging report of what he had witnessed.

One key characteristic which set Joshua apart from the rest of the Israelites was his level of faith, as he believed the promises of God and refused to be intimidated by the size or strength of the enemy and their cities.

JOSHUA REMEMBERED
HOW THE ALMIGHTY
HAD DEALT WITH EGYPT,
AND HE KNEW
THE LORD COULD
SHOW HIS POWER AGAIN.

Sadly, Moses never set foot in Canaan. Before he died, Moses appointed Joshua to be the leader of the Israelites, instructing him: *"Be strong and of good courage; for you shall bring the children of Israel into the land which I swore to them, and I will be with you"* (Deuteronomy 31:21).

This was a heavy responsibility, but with God's help, Joshua was more than ready for the incredible assignment.

As the Israelites came to the banks of the Jordan River, ready to enter Canaan, God parted the waters for Joshua just as He had for Moses at the Red Sea.

SHOUTING TIME!

The biggest conflict remained ahead on the horizon: taking the city of Jericho. With Joshua in command, Jericho was under siege but the walls seemed too strong to be penetrated. That's where the power of God made an unforgettable appearance.

The Lord promised Joshua and the children of Israel that Jericho would be theirs—and then He revealed the plan. God said that Israel's army should *"march around the city ... This you shall do six days. And seven priests shall bear seven trumpets of rams' horns before the ark. But the seventh day you shall march around the city seven times, and the priests shall blow the trumpets"* (Joshua 6:3-4).

Then the Lord instructed that when the priest made a long blast with the ram's horn, and when the Israelites heard the sound of the trumpet, *"all the people shall shout with a great shout; then the wall of the city will fall down flat. And the people shall go up every man straight before him"* (verse 5).

It happened exactly as God promised. The walls of Jericho came crashing down and the Israelites marched right in.

God's General

This was the first of many campaigns which resulted in Joshua conquering the land that the Lord vowed they would live in.

The Bible records that six nations and 31 kings fell to the army which Joshua raised up and commanded. Then, when Canaan was completely subdued, he divided the land according to the tribes and kept Timnath Serah in the mountains of Ephraim as his personal inheritance (Joshua 19:15).

As a military leader, Joshua is considered by many to be one of the greatest generals of all time. One must ask what made this leader, or any leader, truly great. What would have been the outcome without God's intervention? How could he have led the people without divine guidance?

> THIS LEADER
> SET AN EXAMPLE
> OF GREATNESS
> BY HIS DECISION
> TO FOLLOW GOD
> AND HIS DIVINE VOICE.

Whatever giants you are facing today, remember that God is omnipotent and faithful to keep His promises. His favor rests upon those who choose to focus on God rather than on their circumstances.

chapter 8

God's Presence *and* Power *on* DEBORAH

The next time someone tries to tell you that women are weak, tell them to open their Bible and read about a woman named Deborah.

In the book of Judges, you will find that this extraordinary individual had three roles in God's Kingdom—that of a prophetess, a warrior, and a judge. In fact, she is the only female judge mentioned in the Bible. Scripture describes how *"she would sit under the palm tree ... in the mountains of Ephraim. And the children of Israel came up to her for judgement"* (Judges 4:5).

At the time, the enemies of Israel, led by

Jabin, king of Canaan, were gathering to make war. God gave Deborah a word of prophecy, so she called for Barak, a Hebrew military commander, and told him, *"Has not the Lord God of Israel commanded, 'Go and deploy troops at Mount Tabor; take with you ten thousand men of the sons of Naphtali and of the sons of Zebulun; and against you I will deploy Sisera, the commander of Jabin's army, with his chariots and his multitude at the River Kishon; and I will deliver him into your hand'?"* (verses 6-7).

BARAK KNEW THIS WAS MORE THAN A WOMAN SPEAKING; IT WAS A DIRECT COMMAND FROM GOD HIMSELF.

So he replied to Deborah, *"If you will go with me, then I will go; but if you will not go with me, I will not go!"* (verse 8).

It was unprecedented that the leader of an

army would refuse to march into battle unless a woman was by his side, but he recognized that God was with her. Deborah personally accompanied Barak to Mount Tabor, where they were joined by 10,000 troops. When she gave the signal, the army of Israel stormed into battle. Just as Deborah had prophesied, the enemy was completely defeated. This was the first major victory for Israel since the days of Joshua.

Time to Sing

When the conflict ceased, Deborah and Barak wrote a song of praise and sang it together. It is recorded in Judges 5 as "The Song of Deborah."

The words include:

"When leaders lead in Israel,

When the people willingly offer themselves,

Bless the Lord!

Hear, O kings! Give ear, O princes!

I, even I, will sing to the Lord;

I will sing praise to the Lord God of Israel ...

Thus let all Your enemies perish, O Lord!

But let those who love Him be like the sun

When it comes out in full strength."

After the swords and shields were laid down, *"the land had rest for forty years"* (Judges 5:31).

A Breakthrough Anointing

Deborah embodied many qualities that women everywhere would be wise to emulate. She was not only full of passion and valor, she knew God intimately as an intercessor and worshiper. It is important to note that Deborah possessed a breakthrough anointing that allowed people to be set free. This is an anointing that all men and women should seek after.

Women are an incredible force when they tap into God's power and presence. In my travels around the world, I have seen the Lord use women to bring healing, deliverance, and the message of Christ to those who are hurting and without hope.

Today, I encourage women everywhere to stand in the gap for their brothers and sisters in the Lord as well as for those who have lost their way.

YOUR SPIRITUAL STRENGTH
IS CRITICAL TO SOMEONE
IN HIS OR HER MOMENT
OF DESPERATE NEED.
IT IS TIME TO LAY HOLD
OF THE FAITH, AUTHORITY,
AND VALOR OF DEBORAH.

chapter 9

God's Presence and Power on
SAMUEL

A woman named Hannah was extremely distraught. All of her friends were having children, but her womb remained barren. Year after year she went to the temple, crying and weeping to the Lord, pleading with Him to give her a son.

One day, Eli the priest was sitting at the door of the temple and heard her plea. Hannah *was in bitterness of soul, and prayed to the Lord and wept in anguish. Then she made a vow and said, 'O Lord of hosts, if You will indeed look on the affliction of Your maidservant ... but will give Your maidservant a male child, then I will give him to the Lord all the days of his life, and no razor shall come upon his head'"* (1 Samuel 1:11).

At first, the priest thought she was intoxicated, but soon he realized she was sincere in her prayer. Eli told her, *"Go in peace, and [may] the God of Israel grant your petition which you have asked of Him"* (verse 17).

In the process of time, Hannah conceived and bore a son. *"[She] called his name Samuel, saying 'Because I asked for him from the Lord'"* (verse 20).

After Samuel was weaned, Hannah and her husband took the child to the temple and literally gave him to the Lord. Not merely symbolically, but physically—to be raised in the temple by Eli the priest. Hannah said, *"As long as he lives, he shall be lent to the Lord"* (verse 28). This was the same temple where the Ark of the Covenant rested.

Scripture records that *"the child Samuel grew in stature, and in favor with both the Lord and men"* (1 Samuel 2:26).

The Call

One night, while he was still a boy, he heard a voice call out, *"Samuel, Samuel!"*

He woke up and answered, "Yes. I am here." Then he ran to Eli, saying, *"I heard you calling. I'm here."*

Eli told him to go back to sleep because he hadn't awakened him. This happened three times—but it was not Eli, it was the voice of God.

The Lord told Samuel that there was sin in Eli's family and that he would be raised up to lead Israel. As time passed, the Lord began revealing Himself to Samuel, and Israel embraced him as both a prophet and the ruler of that nation.

Under Samuel's leadership, the Israelites turned away from idolatry. At a crucial point, the Philistines stole the Ark of the Covenant. Samuel led the nation of Israel to a triumphant victory over the Philistines—this resulted in the Ark being returned.

Sadly, Samuel's two sons did not follow in their father's footsteps, and Israel couldn't bear the thought of them ruling the nation. So instead of having a prophet for their leader, they demanded a king.

When Samuel heard this, his heart was crushed, but God let him know, *"Heed the voice of the people in all that they say to you; for they have not rejected you, but they have rejected Me"* (1 Samuel 8:7).

A short while later, a young man from the tribe of Benjamin came into the town where Samuel lived while helping his friend look for his lost donkeys. His name was Saul.

The moment Samuel laid eyes on Saul, God said, *"There he is, the man of whom I spoke to you. This one shall reign over My people"* (1 Samuel 9:17).

The Lord works in mysterious ways, His wonders to perform, and Saul was anointed king over Israel. But as we learn in the next chapter, God wasn't finished moving in the life of His servant Samuel.

chapter 10

God's Presence and Power on
DAVID

God gave the people of Israel what they wanted —a king. But Saul turned out to be foolish and corrupt.

THIS IS WHERE
THE HAND OF GOD
MOVED EVEN MORE
AND USED SAMUEL
IN A REMARKABLE WAY.

In Bethlehem there lived a man named Jesse, the great-grandson of Boaz and Ruth. He fathered eight sons, the youngest of whom was

David. David was a shepherd boy who learned and sharpened his fighting skills while protecting his flock from preying animals. In the fields, David also had time to develop his musical talents as he played the flute and harp.

The Lord sent Samuel to the house of Jesse to choose one of his sons as the future king. After interviewing and rejecting the first seven, Samuel asked, *"Are all the young men here?"* Jesse replied, *"There remains yet the youngest, and there he is, keeping the sheep"* (1 Samuel 16:11).

Immediately, God sanctioned His approval of the young man. *"Samuel took the horn of oil and anointed him in the midst of his brothers; and the Spirit of the Lord came upon David from that day forward"* (verse 13).

King Saul suffered from depression, so he asked his servants to find anyone who could sooth his spirit by playing music. You guessed it: they found David who, in turn, spent many days playing the harp for troubled Saul.

Sometime later, in a battle with the Philistines, a giant named Goliath taunted Saul's armies, saying, *"Send one of your men to fight me."* No one was brave enough. Then David came out to see what was going on. Surprisingly, he volunteered. Saul laughed—and so did the giant—but David put a stone in his slingshot and killed Goliath on the spot.

Because of his act of heroism, David was so celebrated in the land that Saul became jealous and tried to kill him. Eventually Saul died in battle, and David became king at the age of 30. He reigned 40 years.

A RENEWED SPIRIT

One of the highlights of his rule was capturing Jerusalem, which he made the capital city of Israel. Three months later, David brought the Ark of the Covenant to the Holy City, which triggered one of the greatest celebrations recorded in Scripture. It was placed in a new Tabernacle that King David built.

The highs and lows of David's life fill many pages of God's Word, including his victorious battles which stand in stark contrast to his sin with Bathsheba. In the midst of David's ups and downs, God called him *"a man after My own heart"* (Acts 13:22).

THE REASON DAVID BECAME SUCH AN INSTRUMENT IN THE HAND OF THE LORD IS BECAUSE HE SOUGHT AFTER THE THINGS OF GOD.

WHEN HE MADE MISTAKES, HE PRAYED FOR FORGIVENESS.

In Psalms 51:1-2 he prays: *"Have mercy upon me, O God, according to your lovingkindness; according to the multitude of Your tender mercies, blot out my transgressions. Wash me thoroughly from my iniquity, and cleanse me from my sin."*

At one point he looked up to the heavens and pleaded, *"Create in me a clean heart, O God, and renew a steadfast spirit within me. Do not cast me away from Your presence, and do not take Your Holy Spirit from me"* (verses 10-11).

In the New Testament, Jesus is called *"The son of David."* Christ's lineage is traced back to David in the first chapter of Matthew.

In many ways, David's life foreshadowed the life of Christ. They were both born in the city of Bethlehem and were shepherds tending their flock (Jesus being called *"The good shepherd"* in John 10:11).

Above all else, David was one who worshiped and loved the Lord. In the Psalms, David has left us with a beautiful collection of songs and prayers of worship. With him we can lift our voices and say, "Praise the Lord!"

chapter 11

God's Presence *and* Power *on*
ELIJAH

Israel was in dire straits when the prophet Elijah came on the scene. King Ahab and his wicked wife, Jezebel, led the country into Baal worship. The Bible tells us, *"Ahab did more to provoke the Lord God of Israel to anger than all the kings of Israel who were before him"* (1 Kings 16:33). Elijah warned of the ominous consequences awaiting them if this pagan worship continued.

Next, we find the prophet at a ravine called Cherith where he was fed by ravens. Then, when the brook dried up, the Lord told him, *"Arise, go to Zarephath, which belongs to Sidon, and dwell*

there. See, I have commanded a widow there to pro-
vide for you" (1 Kings 17:9).

At the city gate, the famished Elijah saw the woman and asked her for a cup of water and a morsel of food. The widow answered that she had only a handful of flour in a bin and a scant amount of oil in a jar. She explained to him, *"I am gathering a couple of sticks that I may go in and prepare it for myself and my son, that we may eat it, and die"* (verse 12).

God instructed the prophet to ask her to go home and make him a small cake first and then she would also have enough for herself and her son, *"For thus says the Lord God of Israel: 'The bin of flour shall not be used up, nor shall the jar of oil run dry, until the day the Lord sends rain on the earth'"* (verse 14).

A miracle was in the making! It happened just as God predicted.

Soon after, the widow's son died from an illness. Elijah literally laid his body over the dead boy and cried, *"O Lord my God, I pray, let this child's soul come back to him"* (verse 21).

God heard the prophet's prayer and her son came back to life.

THE SHOWDOWN

About three years later, Elijah had another confrontation with King Ahab. This time it was on Mount Carmel between himself and 450 pagan prophets of Baal.

The dispute was to determine whose God was actually real.

At the altar of sacrifice, each side was given a bull to cut up and place on the wood, but both were told not to light a fire underneath. Elijah said, *"Then you call on the name of your gods, and I will call on the name of the Lord; and the God who answers by fire, He is God"* (1 Kings 18:24).

When it was Elijah's turn, he poured water on the altar to make it even more difficult. Then he offered this heartfelt prayer: *"Lord God of Abraham, Isaac, and Israel, let it be known this day that You are God in Israel and I am Your servant, and that I have done all these things at Your word. Hear me, O Lord, hear me, that this people may know that You are the Lord God, and that You have turned their hearts back to You again"* (verses 36-37).

WHAT RESULTED WAS A SUPERNATURAL DEMONSTRATION OF THE POWER OF ALMIGHTY GOD.

The fire fell and consumed the offering! It led to the people turning their backs on idolatry and they began worshiping the true Lord.

When Jezebel learned that her priests had been killed at the confrontation, she ordered for Elijah to be murdered.

In fear of his life, the prophet fled. Exhausted,

sleeping under a bush, an angel appeared and offered him nourishment. This miraculous intervention gave him the strength to walk 40 days as he journeyed to Mount Horeb.

The Spirit of Elijah

In the New Testament, it was said about John, the forerunner of the Messiah: *"He will also go before Him* [Jesus] *in the spirit and power of Elijah, 'to turn the hearts of the fathers to the children,' and the disobedient to the wisdom of the just, to make ready a people prepared for the Lord"* (Luke 1:17).

I thank God for His all-consuming fire and power that is available to all who believe in Him.

chapter 12

God's Presence and Power on
ELISHA

The prophet Elijah was walking from Sinai to Damascus when he spotted Elisha working in the fields, ploughing with a yoke of 12 oxen. God had previously told the prophet that this was the man who would one day take his place. Elijah walked over *and threw his mantle on him* (1 Kings 19:19). This was a symbolic gesture—indicating that Elisha would become his successor.

As a signal that a new future was on the horizon, Elisha prepared a barbecue of the oxen, had a banquet for his friends and family. After the feast, he left to become Elijah's servant.

Several years later, when Elijah knew his life on earth was drawing to a close, at Gilgal, the prophet told Elisha, *"'Stay here, please, for the Lord has sent me on to Bethel.' But Elisha said, 'As the Lord lives, and as your soul lives, I will not leave you!' So they went down to Bethel"* (2 Kings 2:2).

The same thing occurred at Bethel and at Jericho. Elisha would not leave the side of Elijah. They were inseparable, so the two of them journeyed ahead.

Upon reaching the banks of the Jordan River, *"Elijah took his mantle, rolled it up, and struck the water; and it was divided this way and that, so that the two of them crossed over on dry ground"* (verse 8).

Finally, Elijah asked Elisha, *"What can I do for you, before I am taken from you?"*

Elisha humbly answered, *"Please let a double portion of your spirit be upon me"* (verse 9).

The prophet responded, *"You have asked a hard thing. Nevertheless, if you see me when I am taken from you, it shall be so for you"* (verse 10).

As they continued walking along together, suddenly a chariot of fire appeared with horses of fire and separated the two men—and Elijah went up to Heaven in a whirlwind.

With his own eyes Elisha saw what was taking place and cried out, *"My father, my father, the chariot of Israel and its horsemen!"* (verse 12)—and saw the prophet no more.

At that moment, Elisha took hold of his own clothes and tore them into two pieces. He also picked up the mantle of Elijah that had fallen from him and went back and stood near the bank of the Jordan.

One key question remained. Would the power that once rested on Elijah now be upon Elisha? What happened next answers that question. The Bible records that Elisha *"took the mantle of Elijah that had fallen from him, and struck the water, and said, 'Where is the Lord God of Elijah?' And when he also had struck the water, it was divided this way and that; and Elisha crossed over"* (verse 14).

"Thus Says the Lord"

This was the beginning of the miracle ministry of the new prophet Elisha.

When he returned to Jericho, the minute the sons of the prophets saw him, they shouted, *"The spirit of Elijah rests on Elisha"* (verse 15). They could see it and feel it, and they bowed to the ground before him.

The water in the city of Jericho was so polluted that people were falling sick and dying. Also, because of the contamination, the crops failed to grow. At the Lord's command, Elisha went to the source of the water, threw in some salt, and declared, *"Thus says the Lord: 'I have healed this water; from it there shall be no more death or barrenness"* (verse 21).

The city's supply of water was made clean.

One day, a man brought Elisha the *"first fruits"* of the barley bread he was making. The prophet instructed, *"Give it to the people that they may eat."*

The man responded, *"What? Shall I set this before one hundred men?"* (verse 43).

Elisha repeated his words, *"The Lord said, 'Do it!'"*

The baker honored the request as he set the few loaves of bread before the one hundred men, *"and they ate and had some left over, according to the word of the Lord"* (verse 44).

IN CASE YOU DIDN'T KNOW, GOD IS STILL IN THE MIRACLE-WORKING BUSINESS.

Elisha left us with a powerful picture of all that can result from one person who is hungry enough to cry out for a double portion of the Holy Spirit. Don't hesitate. Fall on your knees now in the spirit of Elisha and watch as the Lord honors this desire of your heart.

God's Presence *and* Power *on*
NEHEMIAH

Jerusalem had a serious problem. When King Nebuchadnezzar destroyed the city about 150 years earlier, he not only knocked down the walls, but he also burned the gates of the city.

After the Babylonian exile, when the Israelites first came home, they did not repair the shattered walls. This caused the residents to worry about their safety, especially because an enemy could easily launch an attack.

An exiled Jew, still living in Babylon, was a man named Nehemiah. One day, his brother Hanani and some other men from Israel came for a visit. While there, they told him, *"The survivors who are left from the captivity in the province are there in great distress and reproach. The wall of Jerusalem is also broken down, and its gates are burned with fire"* (Nehemiah 1:3). Nehemiah was so saddened by the news that he sat down and cried. Then he began fasting and praying about the situation.

Soon after, the king asked Nehemiah, *"Why are you looking so sad?"*

Nehemiah replied, *"Why should my face not be sad, when the city, the place of my fathers' tombs, lies in waste, and its gates are burned with fire?"* (Nehemiah 2:3).

"What is it that you want?" the king inquired.

Nehemiah answered, *"If it pleases the king, and if your servant has found favor in your sight, I ask that you send me to Judah, to the city of my fathers' tombs, that I may rebuild it"* (verse 5).

The king not only approved but also helped him with supplies for part of the reconstruction.

Spears and Swords

When Nehemiah arrived in Jerusalem, he surveyed the damage. Then, when he announced his plans, the people gave him an enthusiastic response: *"Let's rise up and build"* (Nehemiah 2:18).

In stark contrast, there were enemies of the Israelites living nearby. When they saw portions of the wall being built, they conspired, *"We will go up and kill them and stop the building."*

Nehemiah heard about the threat and armed the workers with spears and swords in preparation for a possible enemy attack. He encouraged the laborers: *"Do not be afraid of them. Remember the Lord, great and awesome, and fight for your brethren, your sons, your daughters, your wives, and your houses"* (Nehemiah 4:14).

Scripture tells us, *"Those who built on the wall, and those who carried burdens, loaded themselves so that with one hand they worked at construction, and with the other held a weapon. Every one of the builders had his sword girded at his side as he built"* (verses 17-18).

The brave volunteers kept their weapons on the ready while they toiled. In a task that should have taken much longer, the walls were finished in just 52 days.

Soon, men and women arrived from all over the region to *"celebrate the dedication with gladness ... with thanksgiving and singing, with cymbals and stringed instruments and harps"* (Nehemiah 12:27).

What About You?

This story illustrates the influence which one person who hears from God can have on a city or even a nation. The Lord doesn't only use preachers or prophets to bring about change and fulfill His plans. Nehemiah held a secular office in Persia, yet the Lord called him to a special assignment of great significance.

What is He asking of you?

God's Presence *and* Power *on* ESTHER

The power of God knows no limits. It can heal the sick, deliver the oppressed, and change the course of history. Here, we see how one Jewish girl was used by God to save an entire nation!

In the time of Babylon, King Xerxes was the ruler. One night, at a party, the king ordered his wife, Queen Vashti, to make an appearance. The king wanted to show everyone how beautiful she was. She refused, and Xerxes was more than upset.

One of the king's advisors, Haman, teased him that if people found out, they would think he had lost his authority at home. So, at Haman's urging, the king had Vashti banished from the palace. In one moment, she lost her husband and her role as queen.

To fill the position vacated by Vashti's departure, the king ordered a search throughout the kingdom for a beautiful girl to be the next queen. Many girls were recruited, but one stood out among the rest. The scouts found a kind, gracious girl named Esther, and soon they were married.

Esther was Jewish. Her family had been driven out of Israel about 70 years prior and were living in exile in Persia—they prayed every day that they would someday be able to return to their homeland.

For Such a Time as This

Esther had an uncle named Mordecai, who encouraged her to hide her faith from her husband—which she did.

By this time, Haman had risen to power in the kingdom. This prideful ruler thought everyone should bow down to him. When Mordecai refused, he asked the king to issue a decree which called for total annihilation of the Jews.

Mordecai found out about this and sent Esther a message about the plot. Even though she was the queen, she could not see the king without being specifically invited. So, after fasting and praying for three days, she took an unthinkable risk. She risked her own life by going to see Xerxes.

Mordecai had told her, *"Who knows whether you have come to the kingdom for such a time as this?"* (Esther 4:14).

The king did not order for Esther to be killed. Instead, at their meeting, the king offered *"half of my kingdom for your wishes."* The queen had found favor with her king.

She responded with an unusual request. All she asked was that the king and Haman join her for dinner that night. At the banquet, the king inquired of her, *"Tell me, what is your request?"*

She put off answering until the three of them shared another meal the next night. Just before the second event, Haman saw Mordecai at the palace gate. When he still refused to bow, Haman was so enraged that he had gallows built on which he planned to hang Mordecai the next day.

That same night the king was restless and unable to sleep, so he asked to read the book that contained the record of his reign. He turned to a page where Mordecai had exposed a conspiracy to assassinate him, thereby saving his life. When he was reminded of this, he asked, *"What reward has Mordecai received?"* He was told that nothing had been done, so he started making plans.

In an ironic twist, the next morning when Haman was arriving at the palace to ask that Mordecai be hanged, King Xerxes greeted him with,

"What should be done for the man the king delights to honor?"

Arrogantly, Haman thought the king was referring to him, so he replied, *"Such a man should be given a royal robe and be led by the king through the streets."*

What a shock it was to Haman when the king ordered: *"Go at once and get the robe and horse and do as you suggest for Mordecai the Jew, who sits at the gate."* Can you imagine all that went through the mind of this evil man who was now ordered to show honor to the same man he planned to murder?

Haman had no other choice but to obey.

Finally, Esther shared the secret that she was a Jew, then begged her husband to spare her people.

When the king found out that Haman had built gallows to hang Mordecai, he was so furious that he ordered Haman to be hanged there instead.

GOD WAS WORKING
SO POWERFULLY
BEHIND THE SCENE
THAT THE KING ISSUED
A NEW ORDER THAT ALL
JEWS IN THE NATION WERE
TO NOT ONLY BE SPARED,
BUT ALSO PROTECTED
AND HONORED.

To this day, Israel lauds Esther with an annual Feast of Purim.

The story of Esther is a powerful illustration of the potential held within each person's God-given destiny. Esther's refusal to give up hope for her people and her incredible selflessness remind us what it looks like to conduct ourselves in a royal manner that honors the one true King.

Imagine the influence your life will have for the Kingdom of God as you seek to live in step with the heartbeat of the one true King of kings.

chapter 15

God's Presence *and* Power *on* JOB

If anybody really "had it made," it was a fellow named Job in the Old Testament. He had a large family, thousands of sheep and oxen, and enormous wealth. He was blessed beyond measure. Some have suggested that, at the time, he was the richest man on earth. The Bible records, *"This man was the greatest of all the people of the East"* (Job 1:3).

Evidently, this really bothered satan. When the devil came to God, the Lord started bragging on His servant Job: *"Have you considered My servant Job, that there is none like him on the earth, a blameless and upright man, one who fears God and shuns evil?"* (verse 8).

Tauntingly, satan thought he'd test the Lord by suggesting that God had put a hedge of protection around Job and blessed him. An unthinkable challenge followed when satan remarked, *"But now, stretch out Your hand and touch all that he has, and he will surely curse You to Your face!"* (verse 11).

THE LORD DECIDED TO PROVE TO THE DEVIL THAT JOB WAS NOT A RIGHTEOUS MAN JUST BECAUSE HE WAS BLESSED AND HAD FAVOR.

So, God replied to satan with His own challenge: *"Behold, all that he has is in your power; only do not lay a hand on his person"* (verse 12). In other words, "I am going to turn him over to you for a while to prove that his faith can't be shaken."

It was then that Job lost it all—his animals, his servants, and his children. Amazingly, one thing remained steadfast, his faith in God.

TOTAL TRUST

I don't know how you would respond to such tragic circumstances, but Job fell to the ground and worshiped the Lord. Here are his words: *"Naked I came from my mother's womb, and naked shall I return there. The Lord gave, and the Lord has taken away; blessed be the name of the Lord"* (verse 21).

Job's wife tried to entice him to *"curse God and die"* (Job 2:9), but he wasn't about to listen to her advice.

Some of Job's friends tried to console him but before long started blaming him for his own problems, even suggesting that he must have sinned terribly for all of these hardships to fall upon him. I'm sure you have encountered people like that.

Despite the ordeal that satan put Job through, he clung to his faith. Job believed that God was more powerful than his circumstances. From the depths of his soul he declared, *"Though He slay me, yet will I trust Him"* (Job 13:15).

A DOUBLE PORTION

I love the end of this remarkable story. God rewarded Job for his faithfulness in all the hardship and suffering which he had endured. Scripture records, *"The Lord restored Job's losses ... [and] gave Job twice as much as he had before"* (Job 42:10). Instead of 7,000 sheep, now he had 14,000. Instead of 500 yoke of oxen, now he had 1,000.

The Lord also honored Job's desire for a family, giving him seven sons and three daughters. We are told, *"After this, Job lived one hundred and forty years, and saw his children and grandchildren for four generations. So Job died, old and full of days"* (verses 16-17).

Friend, I don't know what trials you may be facing or how the enemy is testing you, but I want to encourage you to hold on!

THE LORD HAS INCREDIBLE BLESSINGS IN STORE FOR THOSE WHO ENDURE TO THE END.

GOD WILL REWARD YOU ABUNDANTLY.

The Apostle Paul states it best: *"I consider that the sufferings of this present time are not worthy to be compared with the glory which shall be revealed in us"* (Romans 8:18).

Praise His name!

chapter 16

God's Presence and *Power* on
ISAIAH

In the year that King Uzziah died, a man named Isaiah had a powerful vision. Here is how he described what God revealed to him: *"I saw the Lord sitting on a throne, high and lifted up, and the train of His robe filled the temple. Above it stood seraphim; each one had six wings: with two he covered his face, with two he covered his feet, and with two he flew. And one cried to another and said: 'Holy, holy, holy is the Lord of hosts; The whole earth is full of His glory!'"* (Isaiah 6:1-3). In addition, the posts of the door were shaken by the voice of the One who cried out, and the house was filled with smoke.

This encounter unsettled Isaiah, who responded, *"Woe is me, for I am undone! Because I am a man of unclean lips, and I dwell in the midst of a people of unclean lips; for my eyes have seen the King, the Lord of hosts"* (verse 5).

At that moment, one of the seraphim flew to Isaiah, having in his hand a live coal which he had taken with tongs from off the altar. He touched Isaiah's mouth with it and said, *"Behold, this has touched your lips; your iniquity is taken away, and your sin purged"* (verse 7).

Isaiah was a new man—forgiven by God.

But the question facing Israel concerned finding a replacement for King Uzziah. He had ruled over the kingdom of Judah for 52 years and was considered one of the good monarchs.

Isaiah heard the voice of the Lord saying, "Whom shall I send, and who will go for Us?" (verse 8).

That question struck Isaiah's heart like an arrow. Because God had done such a work in his life, he was ready to do whatever the Lord asked of him. So, Isaiah replied, *"Here I am, send me!"*

Isaiah became one of the heralded Old Testament prophets. This resulted in the prophet being led by God to produce anointed writings which still impact the world today.

A Powerful, Prophetic Word

The presence of the Lord was so evident on Isaiah that God entrusted him to prophesy concerning Jesus Christ coming to earth and dying on the cross for the sins of man.

In the remarkable book that bears his name, Isaiah wrote:

He will be born of a virgin
(Isaiah 7:14; Luke 1:26-31).

He will have a Galilean ministry
(Isaiah 9:1-2; Matthew 4:13-16).

He will be an heir to the throne of David
(Isaiah 40:3-5; Luke 1:32-33).

He will be spat on and struck
(Isaiah 50:6; Matthew 26:67).

He will be disfigured by suffering
(Isaiah 53:14; Mark 15:15-19).

He will make a blood atonement
(Isaiah 53:5; 1 Peter 1:2).

He will be our substitute
(Isaiah 53:6, 8; Romans 5:6).

He will heal the brokenhearted
(Isaiah 61:1-2; Luke 4:18-19).

He will be buried in a rich man's tomb
(Isaiah 53:9; Matthew 27:57-60).

He will judge the world with righteousness
(Isaiah 11:4-5; John 5:27).

I pray you will let the words of Isaiah soak in and speak to your soul. The Lord is patiently waiting to say, "I will pour water on him who is thirsty, and floods on the dry ground; I will pour My Spirit on your descendants, and My blessing on your offspring" (Isaiah 44:3).

If you are burdened and need a special touch from the Lord, claim this promise: *"His burden will be taken away from your shoulder, and his yoke from your neck, and the yoke will be destroyed because of the anointing"* (Isaiah 10:17).

DO YOURSELF A HUGE FAVOR
AS YOU RECALL
THE LIFE OF ISAIAH:
WHEN THE LORD CALLS
YOUR NAME, ANSWER,
"HERE I AM. SEND ME!"

Your life will be forever enriched as you search out Heaven's unique assignment and anointing.

chapter 17

God's Presence *and* Power *on*
JEREMIAH

If you don't think God knows us from beginning to end, take a good look at the life of the prophet Jeremiah.

While he was still young, the Almighty spoke directly to him, saying, *"Before I formed you in the womb I knew you; before you were born I sanctified you; I ordained you a prophet to the nations"* (Jeremiah 1:5).

How did he respond? *"Ah, Lord God! Behold, I cannot speak, for I am a youth"* (verse 6).

His immaturity made no difference to his

Maker. As Jeremiah tells it: *"But the Lord said to me: 'Do not say, "I am a youth," for you shall go to all to whom I send you, and whatever I command you, you shall speak. Do not be afraid of their faces, for I am with you to deliver you"* (verses 7-8).

It was during Jeremiah's ministry that the long missing Book of Law was discovered hidden in Jerusalem's temple (2 Kings 22:3-8). This prophet devoted his life to proclaiming the words found in this Book.

The Lord specifically told him, *"Hear the words of this covenant, and speak to the men of Judah and to the inhabitants of Jerusalem; and say to them, 'Thus says the Lord God of Israel: "Cursed is the man who does not obey the words of this covenant which I commanded your fathers in the day I brought them out of the land of Egypt"* (Jeremiah 11:2-4).

He also made sure that Passover, a festival of God that had long been forgotten, was observed by Israel once more (2 Kings 23:22-23).

LIKE A FIRE

Jeremiah was preaching to a nation that had not only strayed off course … they were practicing rituals that were an abomination. God was angry that they had built altars *"to burn their sons and their daughters in the fire, which I did not command, nor did it come into My heart"* (Jeremiah 7:31). In addition, the people no longer respected the Sabbath day (Jeremiah 17:21-24).

The chief governor caught wind of what Jeremiah was prophesying *"and put him in stocks"* (Jeremiah 20:2).

The prophet was dismayed, moaning, *"I am in derision daily; everyone mocks me"* (verse 7).

He thought about the hardship and contemplated quitting. He may have felt tempted to never mention the name of the Lord publicly ever again, but he knew he could not turn his back on his destiny. As Jeremiah writes, *"His word was in my heart like a burning fire shut up in my bones; I was weary of holding it back, and I could not"* (verse 9).

Jeremiah was an eye witness to the siege on Jerusalem. The Lord revealed to him, *"This city shall surely be given into the hand of the king of Babylon's army, which shall take it"* (Jeremiah 38:3).

THE COMING KING

Like Isaiah, Jeremiah prophesied of Jesus: *"Behold, the days are coming,"* says the Lord, *"That I will raise to David a Branch of righteousness; a King shall reign and prosper, and execute judgment and righteousness in the earth. In His days Judah will be saved, and Israel will dwell safely; Now this is His name by which He will be called: The Lord Our Righteousness"* (Jeremiah 23:5-6).

I pray you will be open and willing to let God speak to you through the prophets. What the Lord said many centuries ago is still relevant today: *"For I know the thoughts that I think toward you, says the Lord, thoughts of peace and not of evil, to give you a future and a hope"* (Jeremiah 29:11).

Bask in His promises and His glorious presence.

chapter 18

God's Presence *and* Power *on*
EZEKIEL

If there ever was a man chosen by God to proclaim the Word of the Lord to the children of Israel, it was Ezekiel. He was both a prophet and a priest.

When the Babylonians captured Jerusalem, Ezekiel went into exile with the Israelites as decreed by King Nebuchadnezzar. It was in Babylon where he became a prophet.

The name Ezekiel means "Strengthened by God." This was appropriate considering that the calling and purpose which the Lord had for him required extraordinary strength and courage.

I've met some believers who have a difficult time reading the book of Ezekiel. They wonder, "What's all this stuff about 'wheels in the middle of wheels' and dry bones coming to life?" But hold on. If you skip over Ezekiel, you're missing out on one of the most spiritual Old Testament books.

Here is God's commission to Ezekiel: *"And you, son of man, do not be afraid of them nor be afraid of their words, though briers and thorns are with you and you dwell among scorpions; do not be afraid of their words or dismayed by their looks, though they are a rebellious house. You shall speak My words to them, whether they hear or whether they refuse, for they are rebellious. But you, son of man, hear what I say to you. Do not be rebellious like that rebellious house; open your mouth and eat what I give you"* (Ezekiel 2:6-8).

THE WATCHMAN

At the start of his ministry, he preached judgment on the nation of Judah. Following Jerusalem's destruction, he saw at least a small glimmer of hope for the future.

The Lord told Ezekiel, *"I have made you a watchman for the house of Israel; therefore, you shall hear a word from My mouth and warn them for Me. When I say to the wicked, 'O wicked man, you shall surely die!' and you do not speak to warn the wicked from his way, that wicked man shall die in his iniquity; but his blood I will require at your hand"* (Ezekiel 33:7-8).

Without question, Ezekiel is best known for his vision of the valley of dry bones (Ezekiel 37).

God transported Ezekiel to a desolate location and asked him to speak to the bones—telling them that the Lord would bring them to life just like the Creator breathed life into Adam.

In total obedience Ezekiel preached the message, and the bones not only came together but flesh covered them, and when breath entered, they rose up to form a huge army.

This parallels the house of Israel being in captivity—a state of living death with no hope. But the dry bones reviving signified the Lord's plan for the future restoration of God's chosen people. Some Bible scholars believe that what he described will happen during the millennial reign of Christ on earth.

Free at Last

The last portion of the book of Ezekiel describes the vision God gave him of a restored Israel after the exile. The Lord told him, *"When I have brought them back from the peoples and gathered them out of their enemies' lands, and I am hallowed in them in the sight of many nations, then they shall know that I am the Lord their God, who sent them into captivity among the nations, but also brought them back to their land, and left none of them captive any longer. And I will not hide My face from them anymore; for I shall have poured out My Spirit on the house of Israel"* (Ezekiel 39:27-29).

IF THERE IS ONE MESSAGE
WE CAN GLEAN FROM EZEKIEL,
IT IS THAT WE
MUST NOT BE ASHAMED
TO SPEAK THE TRUTH
OF THE GOSPEL
TO EVERY PERSON WE MEET—
TO THE WEAK,
TO THE STRONG,
TO THE LOWLY,
TO THE HIGH AND MIGHTY.

Will you ask the Lord for an "Ezekiel anointing" on your life?

chapter 19

God's Presence and Power on DANIEL

No doubt about it, the Babylonians were tough customers. Not only did Nebuchadnezzar's army siege Jerusalem and loot the temple built by Solomon. On their way back to Babylon, they took many prisoners. Among them was a teenager named Daniel.

In this foreign country, Daniel was personally chosen to be trained and prepared for service in the King's palace. During this time, Daniel was a standout. What set him apart was his devotion to God and his unfailing observance of Mosaic law. As a result, he gained the confidence and respect of those over him.

Then came a major test. He was asked to interpret the meaning of a dream Nebuchadnezzar had—without even being told what the dream was about!

DANIEL PASSED THE EXAM WITH FLYING COLORS.

As it is written, the king *"fell on his face, prostrate before Daniel, and commanded that they should present an offering and incense to him. The king answered Daniel, and said, 'Truly your God is the God of gods, the Lord of kings, and a revealer of secrets, since you could reveal this secret'"* (Daniel 2:46-47).

Because of his wisdom and abilities, the king promoted Daniel, showered him with many gifts, and made him ruler of the whole province of Babylon, as well as chief administrator over all the wise men of Babylon.

Daniel held this coveted position for several years, but when a new king, Darius, rose up from the ranks, things were dramatically different. Darius's men wanted to get rid of Daniel, so they plotted a trap. Knowing that Daniel prayed to the God of Israel, the king's counselors issued a decree: *"Whoever petitions any god or man for thirty days except you, O king, shall be cast into the den of lions."* Darius signed the order.

Daniel knew about the decree, but at home, *"in his upper room, with his windows open toward Jerusalem, he knelt down on his knees three times that day, and prayed and gave thanks before his God, as was his custom since early days"* (Daniel 6:10).

Daniel was eventually seen breaking the new law, so he was thrown into the lion's den. Those who forced him into the dreaded den failed to take a key reality into account. God was with him there too. Not only did the Lord close the lions' mouths, but when King Darius released him, he issued a new decree: "In every dominion of my kingdom men must tremble and fear before the God of Daniel" (verse 26).

The Revelation

The early days of Daniel set the stage for what was to come. The presence of God was so tangible in his life that the Lord revealed many things to him concerning the end time. What he wrote thousands of years ago reads as if it could belong in the New Testament: *"And there shall be a time of trouble, such as never was since there was a nation, even to that time. And at that time your people shall be delivered, every one who is found written in the book. And many of those who sleep in the dust of the earth shall awake, some to everlasting life, some to shame and everlasting contempt"* (Daniel 12:1-2).

The reason God blessed him with such favor was because of his integrity. He had the respect of the powerful rulers he served, yet he never compromised his faith or his complete trust in the Almighty.

It is not hard to decipher. Daniel's secret can also be yours: If you want to live in the presence of the Lord, obedience to God must always take precedence over obedience to man.

chapter 20

God's Presence and Power on
ZEPHANIAH

The great-great-grandson of Hezekiah was named Zephaniah. Zephaniah led a spiritual revolution to wipe out idol worship from Israel. He became a man of God with the authority to stand before the people and proclaim judgment to a nation that had gone astray—simultaneously, he carried a message of hope for those who would repent.

Zephaniah saw the greatness of God, and it transformed his life. He also understood that the Lord hated a spirit of haughtiness, and that the people needed to recognize their own shortcomings. He tells us, *"Seek the Lord, all you meek of the earth, who have upheld His justice. Seek righteousness, seek humility. It may be that you will be hidden in the day of the Lord's anger"* (Zephaniah 2:3).

Today, there are individuals who make a blatant mockery of worship when they live in open sin. On Sunday they attend church wearing a false face, looking pious. Their behavior the rest of the week, however, tells the real story. Zephaniah lets us know how seriously the Lord takes our lives and our relationship with Him.

What a Day!

The text of Zephaniah mentions "the day of the Lord" more than any other book in the Old Testament. It refers to both Judah's fall to Babylon as well as the eventual judgments and restoration of all things. *"The great day of the Lord is near"* (1:14). God told him, *"I will bring distress upon men, and they shall walk like blind men, because they have sinned against the Lord"* (verse 17).

"The day of the Lord" turns our attention to the earthshaking events that will unfold before the return of Christ. The prophet writes that it will be *"a day of wrath, a day of trouble and distress, a day of devastation and desolation, a day of darkness and gloominess"* (Zephaniah 1:15).

As the Apostle Paul pens much later, *"For you yourselves know perfectly that the day of the Lord so comes as a thief in the night"* (1 Thessalonians 5:2).

Zephaniah points to the amazing changes that will take place at the second coming of Christ. What he talks about under the Spirit's leading is echoed centuries later by Peter when he prayed that God *"may send Jesus Christ, who was preached to you before whom Heaven must receive until the times of restoration of all things, which God has spoken by the mouth of all His holy prophets since the world began"* (Acts 3:20-21).

Jesus Christ alone has the power and authority to initiate and complete the restoration process of the world. The men and women who seek God and trust Him will become part of the remnant who will be examples of righteousness to all mankind. As the prophet writes, *"The remnant of Israel shall do no unrighteousness and speak no lies, nor shall a deceitful tongue be found in their mouth; for they shall feed their flocks and lie down, and no one shall make them afraid"* (Zephaniah 3:12-13).

Ultimate Deliverance

Those who read Zephaniah's words may think they are too harsh—too unforgiving; however, the punishments described would not have to occur if people would respond to God's mandate.

A PRAYER
FOR REPENTANCE
IS THE KEY
TO DELIVERANCE.

Thankfully, all is not lost. The wrath being poured out results in the blessing of God's presence among all believers. He prophesied, *"The Lord your God in your midst, the Mighty One, will save; He will rejoice over you with gladness, He will quiet you with His love, He will rejoice over you with singing"* (Zephaniah 3:17).

The message of Zephaniah includes ultimate deliverance. He speaks of the day when God says, *"I will restore to the peoples a pure language, that they all may call on the name of the Lord, to serve Him with one accord"* (Zephaniah 3:9).

If this prophet placed your life under a microscope, what would he see? Where do you stand? Will you escape the wrath of God? Are you ready and waiting for "the day of the Lord"? For those with humility and a hunger for God's presence, a heart-felt prayer of repentance is often the gateway to deliverance.

chapter 21

God's Presence and Power on
MARY

When Rome ruled Israel, there was a commonplace small town named Nazareth, located about 65 miles north of Jerusalem. Not much out of the ordinary happened there. In fact, a man named Nathaniel asked, *"Can anything good come out of Nazareth?"* (John 1:46).

The answer is a resounding, *"Yes!"* From the womb of a woman who lived there, Mary, was born the greatest Man in history.

The birth of Christ was indeed miraculous. God sent the angel Gabriel to Mary—a virgin engaged to a carpenter in Nazareth named Joseph.

What the angel told her came as a total surprise: *"Rejoice, highly favored one, the Lord is with you: blessed are you among women!"* (Luke 1:28).

What a strange greeting! Then Gabriel continued, *"Do not be afraid, Mary, for you have found favor with God. And behold, you will conceive in your womb and bring forth a Son, and shall call His name Jesus. He will be great, and will be called the Son of the Highest; and the Lord God will give Him the throne of His father David. And He will reign over the house of Jacob forever, and of His kingdom there will be no end"* (verses 30-33).

Mary wondered how this could be since she had never been intimate with Joseph. That's when the angel reassured her, *"The Holy Spirit will come upon you, and the power of the Highest will overshadow you; therefore, also, that Holy One who is to be born will be called the Son of God"* (verse 35).

Mary was nearing the end of her pregnancy when Caesar Augustus issued a decree for a census, and those with a lineage of David had to register in Bethlehem. While taking refuge in a lowly manger there, Jesus was born.

All Heaven and Earth rejoiced! *"And suddenly there was with the angel a multitude of the heavenly host praising God and saying: 'Glory to God in the highest, And on earth peace, goodwill toward men!"* (Luke 2:13-14).

For 30 years, Mary "mothered" Jesus in Nazareth, and Joseph taught Him carpentry skills. They read Scriptures to their Son and He was dedicated in the temple, but Mary could not shrug off what the angel had told her and the many miracles that surrounded His birth—the star, the shepherds, the wise men, and so much more.

When Jesus was just twelve years old, the family traveled to Jerusalem for the Feast of Passover. There He slipped away from His parents and began talking to the priests at the temple. When Mary and Joseph found Him, He asked, *"Why did you seek Me? Did you not know that I must be about My Father's business?"* (verse 49).

A Witness of God's Power

Just before Jesus began His public ministry, at the age of 30, He and Mary were guests at a wedding in Cana. When the hosts ran out of wine, Jesus performed His first miracle. Mary watched in amazement as the water turned to wine!

She was also standing at the foot of the cross when the Son she birthed was brutally crucified. Jesus looked down at Mary and said, *"Woman, behold your son!"* (John 19:26). Then He turned His eyes to the Apostle John, who was standing next to her, *"Behold your mother!"* (verse 27). From that day forward, the disciple took Mary into his own home and looked after her.

The mother of Jesus, Mary, is not to be elevated and worshiped, but loved and honored for her willingness to be a vessel of the Holy Spirit and used of God in bringing His Son to Earth.

Her yielded life reminds us that we are called to be willing vessels of the Holy Spirit, used by God to carry and release His Son.

chapter 22

God's Presence *and* Power *on*
JOHN

What an interesting man. In the desert he ate locusts and honey. Huge crowds followed him, but he downplayed his own importance. He was consistent in revealing that his assignment was to let them know about the coming Messiah.

John the Baptist had a birth so unusual that it is recorded in Scripture. His parents, Zacharias and Elizabeth, had been childless. Scripture tells us, *"Elizabeth was barren, and they were both well advanced in years"* (Luke 1:7).

One day, when Zacharias was worshiping at the temple, he was surprised by the appearance of an angel. The angel told him that his wife would bear a child to be named John, and that *"He will ... be filled with the Holy Spirit, even from his mother's womb. And he will turn many of the children of Israel to the Lord their God"* (verses 15-16).

One of the more fascinating aspects to the story is that Elizabeth and Mary, the mother of Jesus, were related. One day Mary came to visit the pregnant Elizabeth, and *"when Elizabeth heard the greeting of Mary, the babe (John) leaped in her womb, and Elizabeth was filled with the Holy Spirit"* (verse 41). Jesus was born about six months after John.

John's birth was a miracle. There is no doubt that he was placed on earth for a divine purpose. His mission was to preach repentance, baptize people in water, and prepare people for the coming of Jesus.

He wasn't your typical evangelist, as he *"was clothed in camel's hair, with a leather belt around his waist"* (Matthew 3:4). With a loud voice, he went about preaching, *"Repent, for the kingdom of heaven is at hand!"* (verse 2). His role in the King-dom was prophesied by Isaiah when he wrote of, *"The voice of one crying in the wilderness: 'Prepare the way of the Lord'"* (Isaiah 40:3).

John traveled the dusty roads, telling all who would listen, *"He who is coming after me is might-ier than I, whose sandals I am not worthy to carry"* (Matthew 3:11). By the way, the job of carrying sandals was the task of the lowliest slave.

When it was time for Jesus to start His public ministry, He sought out John to baptize Him in the Jordan River. As the Holy Spirit descended on the Lord in the form of a dove, it confirmed to John that this was, indeed, the Son of God (Matthew 3:15-17).

A Tragic End

This forerunner of Christ was rough around the edges and had no qualms calling sin, sin. When he criticized King Herod for marrying his brother's wife, he was thrown into prison (Mark 6:17-18).

While John was behind bars, Herod threw a wild party. Things quickly got out of hand when his wife's daughter danced. He loved her performance so much that he told her, "I'll give you anything you desire."

She replied, "Give me John the Baptist's head here on a platter" (Matthew 14:8). Herod was immediately sorry he ever made such an offer, but an oath is an oath. He ordered John to be killed in jail and "His head was brought on a platter and given to the girl" (verse 11).

The disciples came and took away the body for burial and relayed the tragic news to the Lord.

John's powerful message of repentance and the importance of water baptism is still a foundation of the Christian faith.

Jesus called John "great," but then goes on to say: *"but he who is least in the kingdom of heaven is greater than he"* (Matthew 11:11).

Every wise individual will choose to build their lives upon this timeless teaching.

chapter 23

God's Presence and Power on
JESUS

When you read the Gospels you'll quickly notice that when Christ walked this earth among men He demonstrated a power that came from mirroring His Father in Heaven. Jesus modeled a relationship between Father in Heaven and Son on earth.

Jesus's own words tell the story:

"I and the Father are one" (John 20:30).

"The Son can do nothing of Himself, but what He sees the Father do; for whatever He does, the Son also does in like manner" (John 5:19).

"When you lift up the Son of Man, then you will know that I am He, and that I do nothing of Myself; but as My Father taught Me, I speak these things" (John 8:28).

Leading up to His crucifixion Jesus prayed, "Father, if it is Your will, take this cup away from Me; nevertheless not My will, but Yours be done" (Luke 22:42).

Jesus was a faithful and obedient Son even to death.

POWER OF THE SPIRIT

Jesus walked in the power of the Holy Spirit in His life and ministry.

Acts 10:38 tells us, *"God anointed Jesus of Nazareth with the Holy Spirit and with power, who went about doing good and healing all who were oppressed by the devil, for God was with Him."*

Following His resurrection, Jesus continued to demonstrate on the power of the Holy Spirit. As it is written, *"He was taken up, after He through the Holy Spirit had given commandments to the apostles"* (Acts 1:1-2).

Today, listen to His voice: *"'He who believes in Me ... out of his heart will flow rivers of living water.' But this He spoke concerning the Spirit, whom those believing in Him would receive"* (John 7:38-39).

It's thrilling to know that Jesus promised that we could receive the same Spirit of power that raised Him from the dead: *"But if the Spirit of Him who raised Jesus from the dead dwells in you, He who raised Christ from the dead will also give life to your mortal bodies through His Spirit who dwells in you"* (Romans 8:11).

JESUS DEMONSTRATED A LIFE OF PRAYER

Early in Jesus's ministry we read, *"He went out to the mountain to pray, and continued all night in prayer to God"* (Luke 6:12).

When He walked down from the mountain, a great crowd from Judea, Jerusalem, and other areas *"came to hear Him and be healed of their disease, as well as those who were tormented with unclean spirits"* (verses 17-18).

Notice what happens next. The Bible records, *"And they were healed. And the whole multitude sought to touch Him, for power went out from Him and healed them all"* (verses 18-19).

These great miracles were preceded by Jesus spending the night in prayer, on the mountain, with His Heavenly Father.

Since we are not as strong or wise as Christ, we too must become more dependent on our Heavenly Father to provide all that we need.

This reliance may seem to be a sign of weakness, but, in reality, it is one of strength. It takes plenty of self-control to willingly be dependent on others or on Almighty God.

What an insightful lesson for you and me.

chapter 24

God's Presence and Power on
MATTHEW

There's nothing like having a front row seat to witness the most profound events the earth has ever seen. Yet Matthew was one of just a few who had the privilege of being with Jesus during His three-year ministry.

At the city of Capernaum, Jesus *"saw a man named Matthew sitting at the tax office. And he said to him, 'Follow Me.' So he arose and followed Him"* (Matthew 9:9).

The same encounter is recorded in Luke, but there it uses his former name, Levi. It's not known whether Jesus gave him the name Matthew or if he changed it himself, but it is a shortened version of Matthias—which means "gift of Yahweh," or "the gift of God."

In Luke 5 we find that after the Lord's call, *"Levi gave Him a great feast in his own house. And there were a great number of tax collectors and others who sat down with them. And their scribes and the Pharisees complained against His disciples, saying, 'Why do You eat and drink with tax collectors and sinners?'"* (verses 29-30).

Jesus answered, *"Those who are well have no need of a physician, but those who are sick. I have not come to call the righteous, but sinners, to repentance"* (verses 31-32).

If you took an opinion poll in those days, tax collectors would rate near the bottom. People did their best to avoid them because they were usually dishonest. In many cases the job paid no salary, so they were expected to make their living by cheating those from whom they collected taxes.

It's interesting to note that, since Matthew

came from a financial background, he used more words for money than any other Gospel writer. In fact, the Parable of the Talents is found only in his book.

No Turning Back

From the moment Matthew said "Yes" to the Lord's invitation, he didn't look back. Instead he abandoned a life of riches and security for a future of hardship and uncertainty. He said farewell to the world's pleasures for the promise of eternal life serving Jesus Christ.

What a life it was! He saw God's power and presence in action and faithfully recorded the miracle ministry of Jesus.

Two Blind Men Healed

One day, two blind men followed Jesus, crying out to Him, *"Son of David, have mercy on us!"* (Matthew 9:27).

The Lord replied, *"Do you believe that I am able to do this?"* They answered, *"Yes, Lord."*

Then He touched their eyes, saying, *"'According to your faith let it be to you.' And their eyes were opened"* (verses 29-30).

A Mute Man Speaks

They brought to Jesus a man who was mute and demon possessed. *"And when the demon was cast out, the mute spoke. And the multitudes marveled, saying, 'It was never seen like this in Israel!'"* (Matthew 9:33).

The Cleansing of a Leper

A leper came to Jesus, worshiping Him, pleading, *"Lord, if You are willing, You can make me clean"* (Matthew 8:2).

Jesus reached out His hand and touched him, saying, *"I am willing, be cleansed"* (verse 3).

Immediately, his leprosy vanished and the man was totally healed!

Matthew came a long way from his days spent as a tax collector. He became a devoted disciple of Jesus Christ and the writer of the first book in the New Testament.

The Lord can use anyone to help Him build the Kingdom.

NO ONE SHOULD FEEL DISQUALIFIED BECAUSE OF THEIR BACKGROUND, AGE, APPEARANCE, PAST MISTAKES, OR ANY OTHER FACTOR.

Jesus is only looking for a willing heart and a sincere commitment. It is life's highest calling— and nothing can compare with being a follower of Christ.

Have you answered the call?

chapter 25

God's Presence and Power on
MARK

If you want a fast-paced, exciting glimpse into the life and work of Jesus, read the incredible book of Mark. He starts with the launching of Jesus's ministry and ends with the resurrection and ascension, painting a picture of Jesus as a Servant of God who came to earth to do the will of His Father.

Instead of writing about Jewish genealogies and giving us birth reports, he carries us right into the action and keeps moving rapidly to the end.

In addition, Mark makes Scripture come alive

with exciting, descriptive language. For example:

"They were astonished at His teaching" (Mark 1:22).

"Then they were all amazed, so that they questioned among themselves" (verse 27).

"They feared exceedingly, and said to one another, 'Who can this be, that even the wind and the sea obey Him?" (Mark 4:41).

Mark could write enthusiastically about the power of God for one compelling reason. He had witnessed that power first hand!

A LIFE OF MINISTRY

Who was this man named Mark? In Scripture he is often referred to as John Mark. For instance, in the book of Acts, after Peter was released from prison, we read that *"he came to the house of Mary, the mother of John whose surname was Mark, where many were gathered together praying"* (Acts 12:12).

Later, we find Mark mentioned as a companion of Barnabas and Paul during their travels together (Acts 12:25). John Mark was also Barnabas's cousin (Colossians 4:10).

Mark was far from perfect. In fact, he abandoned Paul on the apostle's first missionary journey when he chose to return home (Acts 13:13). But over time, he grew in the things of the Lord. When Peter was writing from Rome, he affectionately referred to Mark as *"my son"* (1 Peter 5:13). This revealed the depth of relationship which had been built over time.

Later in life, Mark ministered with Paul who calls him a *"fellow laborer"* (Philemon 1:24).

As Paul's life was winding to its conclusion, from a Roman prison, he sent a request to Timothy: *"Get Mark and bring him with you, for he is useful to me for ministry"* (2 Timothy 4:11).

It is obvious that Mark had matured through the years and was a faithful minister of God's Word.

Mark's Themes

Four great themes found in the book of Mark:

1. The Cross

"Whoever desires to come after Me, let him deny himself, and take up his cross, and follow Me" (Mark 8:34).

2. Discipleship

"Jesus said to them, 'Follow Me, and I will make you fishers of men'" (Mark 1:17).

3. The Teachings of Jesus

"And Jesus, when He came out, saw a great multitude and was moved with compassion for them, because they were like sheep not having a shepherd. So He began to teach them many things" (Mark 6:34).

4. The Son of God

"Then a voice came from heaven, 'You are My beloved Son, in whom I am well pleased'" (Mark 1:11).

I hope I've encouraged you to read the entire book of Mark. I believe you will catch the passion of Mark and experience the presence of the Lord.

chapter 26

God's Presence *and* Power *on*
PETER

Of all Christ's apostles, none were as bold or outspoken as Peter. Born into a humble family in the village of Bethsaida, he and his brother, Andrew, became Galilean fishermen.

Before being called as a disciple, however, Peter was ashamed of his past, admitting, *"I am a sinful man, O Lord!"* (Luke 5:8). Yet, Jesus told him, to put down his nets: *"From now on you will catch men"* (verse 10).

Without hesitation, Peter walked away from his boat and left everything to follow Christ.

In those days, fishermen were rough and ready: unkempt, gruff, boisterous, and often using foul language. James and John were also fishermen; perhaps this is why Jesus gave them the names, *"Sons of Thunder"* (Mark 3:17).

As you read the Gospels, you will find Peter as a frequent spokesman for the other disciples. He was the first to call Christ the *"Son of the living God"* (John 6:69).

His original name was Simon, but Jesus changed it to Peter—which means, petra, or "rock." The Lord saw greatness in this man, and declared concerning him, *"On this rock I will build My church, and the gates of Hades shall not prevail against it"* (Matthew 16:18).

Peter saw divine history in the making—Jesus raising a little girl from the dead (Matthew 9:23-26), and Christ walking on the water (Matthew 14:28-29).

Along with James and John, Peter witnessed the Shekinah glory of God on Christ on the

Mount of Transfiguration. Suddenly the face of Jesus *"shone like the sun, and His clothes became white as the light"* (Matthew 17:2).

What a defining moment! Instead of seeing the humanity of Jesus, they saw His divinity.

Then a voice spoke out of the cloud, saying, *"This is My beloved Son, in whom I am well pleased. Hear Him!"* (verse 5).

A Disciple's Denial

Before Christ's arrest and trial, Peter assured Jesus, *"I will lay down my life for Your sake"* (John 13:37). But the Lord knew the impetuous Peter better than he knew himself, and responded, *"The rooster shall not crow till you have denied Me three times"* (verse 38).

Those words became reality.

Later that night, after Jesus was taken into custody, Peter was sitting outside in a courtyard when a servant girl commented, *"You ... were* with *Jesus of Galilee*" (Matthew 26:69). Peter denied it, replying, *"I do not know what you are saying"* (verse 70).

It happened again, when another girl spotted him and said to those present, *"This fellow was also with Jesus of Nazareth"* (verse 71). Once more, Peter swore, *"I do not know the Man"* (verse 72).

Those who gathered around Peter insisted, *"Surely you also are one of them, for your speech betrays you"* (verse 73). For the third time, he began to curse and swear, *"I do not know the Man"* (verse 74).

At that moment, a rooster crowed, and Peter, remembering what Jesus had said, wept bitterly.

During the crucifixion and beyond, God continued to speak to Peter's heart. It was this disciple who was the first to enter the empty tomb (John 20:1-9). And after the resurrection, Jesus appeared to Peter before making Himself known to the other disciples (Luke 24:34).

Before God's Son ascended back to Heaven, He totally restored Peter to ministry (John 20).

It Happened at Pentecost

The major turnaround in the life of Peter took place in the Upper Room on the Day of Pentecost. He and 120 others received what Jesus had promised—the power of the Holy Spirit.

Now a changed man, the disciple walked out of that room and proclaimed Christ with such anointing and authority that during his first sermon alone, 3,000 were saved!

While over one hundred lives were transformed when the Holy Spirit came down into the Upper Room, countless others walked away. The same Holy Spirit is still transforming lives today.

DON'T MISS YOUR OPPORTUNITY TO PRESS INTO CHRIST TO RECEIVE ALL HE HAS WAITING FOR YOU.

chapter 27

God's Presence and Power on
JAMES

On the shores of the Sea of Galilee, after calling Peter and Andrew, Jesus saw two other brothers. James and John were in the boat with their father Zebedee, mending their fishing nets. When Jesus gave them His divine invitation, *"immediately, they left the boat and their father, and followed Him"* (Matthew 4:22).

It's easy to be confused since there are other James's in the early church, including the half-brother of Jesus who wrote the New Testament book of James. But here we are talking about one of the Lord's twelve disciples.

Peter, James, and John were the three who were on the mountain with the Lord when *"Moses and Elijah appeared to them, talking with Him [Jesus]"* (Matthew 17:3).

JAMES WAS PRESENT AT THIS UNPARALLELED MOMENT WHEN GOD'S VOICE BOOMED OUT OF THE CLOUDS, CONFIRMING THAT JESUS TRULY WAS HIS SON (VERSE 5).

The two brothers, James and John, wore their emotions on their sleeves. In one city they were so upset with men and women who didn't accept *Christ as the Messiah that they asked Jesus, "Lord, do You want us to command fire to come down from heaven and consume them, just as Elijah did?"* (Luke 9:54).

Jesus had to calm the pair down and remind them, *"The Son of Man did not come to destroy men's lives but to save them"* (verse 56).

James witnessed one of the greatest miracles recorded in Scripture. One day while Jesus was ministering, a ruler of the synagogue named Jairus fell at the Lord's feet and begged, *"My little daughter lies at the point of death. Come and lay Your hands on her, that she may be healed, and she will live"* (Mark 5:23).

A few minutes later, someone rushed up to Jairus with the news that his daughter had died. Upon hearing this, Jesus immediately headed for the man's house. *"He permitted no one to follow Him except Peter, James, and John"* (verse 37).

Jesus reached out, took the 12-year-old child by the hand, and commanded, *"Little girl, I say to you, arise"* (verse 41). Breath flowed into her lifeless body!

THE SPIRIT SPOKE

In Jesus's darkest hour, who did He take with Him as He prayed in the Garden of Gethsemane? Only Peter, James, and John (Matthew 26:37).

On the Mount of Olives, James heard with his own ears Jesus speaking of the *"signs of the times"* and the end of the age (Mark 13:3-4)—wars and rumors of wars, nations rising against nations, earthquakes, and famines.

Then Jesus told James and the others, when they preached these impending perils, to expect persecution, *"But when they arrest you and deliver you up, do not worry beforehand, or premeditate what you will speak. But whatever is given you in that hour, speak that; for it is not you who speak, but the Holy Spirit"* (verse 11).

James was in the Upper Room when the Holy Ghost fell at Pentecost (Acts 1:13). That's when he received power from on high that catapulted him into an expanded, dynamic ministry.

An Eternal Reward

Stephen, who was ultimately stoned to death, was the first Christian martyr, but James was the first apostle to die a gruesome death. The followers of Christ were multiplying at such a rapid rate that the Roman rulers felt threatened. The Bible records, *"Herod the king stretched out his hand to harass some from the church. Then he killed James the brother of John with the sword"* (Acts 12:1-2).

WHEN JAMES SAID FAREWELL TO THIS EARTH, HIS ETERNAL REWARD WAS AWAITING HIM.

James's example gives us much food for thought and should cause us to evaluate our own lives. Are you willing to follow Jesus to the end as James did regardless of what comes your way? God's power and presence at work in our lives is worth this commitment!

chapter 28

God's Presence and Power on
LUKE

Dr. Luke is mentioned only three times in Scripture (Colossians 4, 2 Timothy 1, and Philemon 1), but out of sight, he was a powerful witness and influence in the early church.

For many reasons, biblical scholars believe that Luke not only wrote the Gospel that bears his name, but also the book of Acts.

As a historian, Luke goes into intricate detail in telling the story of Christ as experienced by eyewitness accounts.

There are several events that appear only in his Gospel, including the background of the birth of

John the Baptist and the account of the two men who met the resurrected Jesus on the road to Emmaus. Without question, Luke has the most detailed description of the birth of Jesus.

Luke's hometown was Antioch, which many scholars believe is the reason it seems to be at the center of much of the book of Acts.

Compassion for the Sick

We know that Luke was a medical doctor. Paul, when writing to the believers at Colossae, gave them greetings from *"Luke the beloved physician"* (Colossians 4:14).

Perhaps it was due to his medical background that Luke includes the most healing stories found in any of the Gospels. This distinction of his writing style also reveals his compassion for the infirmed.

Obviously, Luke was a humble man since he never mentions that he is the author of his books, nor does he refer to his profession as a doctor—but others do. However, his interest in medicine shines through. He is the only Gospel writer who records Jesus's statements concerning doctors: *"Physician, heal yourself"* (Luke 4:23) and *"Those who are well have no need of a physician"* (Luke 5:31).

Luke's major objective and purpose in writing his Gospel was to present the truth concerning Jesus Christ and the plan of salvation. With the guidance of the Holy Spirit, he accomplished that purpose. He focused on the "Good News"— a term that appears ten times in Luke and 12 times in the book of Acts.

It's Prayer Time

When you study the book of Luke, there is no question that he believed in the power of prayer.

When Jesus was baptized: *"… while He prayed, the heaven was opened. And the Holy Spirit descended in bodily form like a dove upon Him"* (Luke 3:21-22).

On the cross, Christ prayed, *"Father, forgive them, for they do not know what they do"* (Luke 23:34).

Before choosing the apostles, *"He went out to the mountain to pray, and continued all night in prayer to God"* (Luke 6:12).

At the transfiguration, *"He took Peter, John, and James and went up on the mountain to pray"* (Luke 9:28).

Jesus taught prayer: *"Now it came to pass, as He was praying in a certain place, when He ceased, that one of His disciples said to Him, 'Lord, teach us to pray'"* (Luke 11:1).

Think for a moment about the life of Luke. After spending years preparing to be a physician and practicing medicine, he willingly gave it up to spend the final years of his life preaching and writing about the Son of God, the Savior of the world.

No matter what course in life you set for yourself, when the Lord has other plans, get ready to change direction! His destiny for your life promises to be more fulfilling than any other path.

chapter 29

God's Presence and Power on
STEPHEN

We meet Stephen for the first time when the early church was growing by leaps and bounds. There was a problem, however, between Greek-speaking and Hebrew-speaking believers regarding discrimination of widows during food handouts.

At an emergency meeting of the twelve disciples, they decided they shouldn't abandon their mission of preaching the Gospel to take care of the poor. So, they asked the church to *"seek out from among you seven men of good reputation, full of the Holy Spirit and wisdom, whom we may appoint over this business; but we will give ourselves* continually to prayer and to the ministry of the word" (Acts 6:3-4).

Stephen was one of those selected. The Bible describes him as *"a man full of faith and the Holy Spirit"* (verse 5).

Stephen's role included much more than taking care of elderly widows. God used him in the miraculous: *"Stephen, full of faith and power, did great wonders and signs among the people"* (verse 8).

But some jealous individuals tried to tear Stephen down, even bribing some men to lie, saying *"We heard him cursing Moses."* As a result, religious leaders grabbed Stephen and took him before the High Council, where even more charges of blasphemy were hurled against him. Yet Scripture records, *"All who sat in the council, looking steadfastly at him, saw his face as the face of an angel"* (verse 15). That was the glow of the Holy Ghost shining through him!

The high priest asked Stephen, *"Are these things they are saying about you true?"*

A Bold Witness

What took place next in the courtroom caught everyone by surprise. Instead of trying to refute the charges, Stephen took the opportunity to present the Gospel of Christ to the large crowd that had gathered—starting with how God called Abraham out of idolatry and ending with the Father sending His Son to die on the cross for the sins of man.

Before finishing his amazing address, Stephen looked at his accusers and boldly charged, *"You stiff-necked and uncircumcised in heart and ears! You always resist the Holy Spirit; as your fathers did, so do you. Which of the prophets did your fathers not persecute? And they killed those who foretold the coming of the Just One, of whom you now have become the betrayers and murderers, who have received the law by the direction of angels and have not kept it"* (Acts 7:51-53).

At that point a full-fledged riot broke out. But Stephen, saturated with the Holy Spirit, hardly noticed. He gazed up and exclaimed, *"Look! I see the heavens opened and the Son of Man standing at the right hand of God!"* (verse 56).

Stephen's voice was drowned out by the mob, who dragged him out of town and pelted him with rocks. The ringleaders asked a young man named Saul to watch them—yes, the same Saul who was a persecutor of Christians.

As they stoned Stephen, he was calling on God, saying, *"Lord Jesus, receive my spirit"* (verse 59). Then he knelt down and praying loud enough so everyone could hear, he cried, *"Lord, do not charge them with this sin"* (verse 60). Those were his last words on earth.

Stephen was not only among the first deacons in the Bible, he was also the first martyr of the Church. His death was overshadowed by his faithfulness, his devotion, and his forgiving spirit.

Take a few moments to remember with honor those who have shed their blood while taking a courageous stand for God and His Kingdom.

chapter 30

God's Presence and Power on PHILIP

There are two men named Philip written about in the New Testament—Philip the Apostle, and Philip the Evangelist. I want to focus on the second.

When the disciples chose seven deacons to serve in the church, with Stephen being one of them, Philip was a member of that anointed group.

Like Stephen, he was so endued with God's power that he went everywhere sharing the message of the Messiah.

In Samaria, men and women hung on his every word and saw miracles in action. During one meeting, *"unclean spirits, crying with a loud voice, came out of many who were possessed; and many who were paralyzed and lame were healed"* (Acts 8:7). There was joy in that city!

Before Philip came to town, there was a man who practiced magic, dazzling the citizens who thought he had supernatural powers.

WHEN PHILIP ARRIVED
PROCLAIMING THE
NAME OF JESUS,
THEY FORGOT ABOUT
THE WIZARD AND WERE
SAVED AND BAPTIZED.

EVEN THE MAGICIAN
WANTED TO BE BAPTIZED!

He wouldn't leave Philip's side, *"amazed [at] seeing the miracles and signs which were done"* (verse 13).

The Spirit Fell!

The exciting news of Philip's impact on Samaria reached Jerusalem. Peter and John rushed over to join Philip and to pray for the converts to receive the gift of the Holy Spirit. Up to this time the believers had only been baptized in water. The apostles *"laid hands on them, and they received the Holy Spirit"* (verse 17).

The magician, spellbound at what was happening, pulled out his money, asking, *"Give me this power also, that anyone on whom I lay hands may receive the Holy Spirit"* (verse 19).

Incensed, Peter severely chastised him: *"Your money perish with you, because you thought that the gift of God could be purchased!"* (verse 20).

Peter told the man to repent. Scripture goes on to reveal that he did.

Climbing in the Chariot

Later, an angel of the Lord spoke to Philip:

"I want you to walk over to that desolate road that spans from Jerusalem down to Gaza." Obedient to the angel, he began the journey.

On the way he met an Ethiopian eunuch who was traveling down the same road. The eunuch had been on a pilgrimage to Jerusalem and was returning to his home country where he was a government official in charge of the finances of Candace, queen of the Ethiopians. Befitting his high rank, he was riding in a chariot and reading the words of the prophet Isaiah.

God's Spirit spoke to Philip: *"'Go near and overtake this chariot.' Philip ran to him, and heard him reading the prophet Isaiah. He asked the poignant question, 'Do you understand what you are reading?'"* (verses 29-30).

He answered, *"How can I without some help?"* In that moment, the eunuch invited Philip into the chariot with him. The passage he was reading continued, *"He was led as a sheep to the slaughter; and as a lamb before its shearer is silent, so He* opened not His mouth. In His humiliation His justice was taken away, and who will declare His generation? For His life is taken from the earth" (verses 32-33).

The eunuch was curious and asked, "Who is the prophet talking about: himself or some other?"

THIS WAS PHILIP'S GOLDEN OPPORTUNITY.

WITH THESE SCRIPTURES AS HIS TEXT, HE EAGERLY PREACHED JESUS, INTRODUCING HIM TO THE ONE TRUE SAVIOR.

As they continued their travels, they came to a stream of water. Upon seeing it the eunuch said, "See, here is water. What hinders me from being baptized?" (verse 36).

Philip told him that if he believed with all his heart, he could.

The man responded, *"I believe that Jesus Christ is the Son of God"* (verse 37). So Philip baptized him right on the spot!

There was one more miracle ahead. The moment they came out of the water, the Spirit of God suddenly carried Philip away (verse 39). That was the last the eunuch saw of him—and the Ethiopian went on his way rejoicing.

The evangelist showed up later on the road to Caesarea, where he continued his ministry with signs and wonders.

What a yielded vessel and marvelous witness Philip was for Christ!

Have you yielded your life to Christ as Philip did? A life surrendered to Jesus is a life of adventure, with the power and presence of God with you every step of the way.

chapter 31

God's Presence *and* Power *on*
PAUL

A young man named Saul was hell bent to create havoc among the followers of this Man called Jesus Christ. In fact, he had permission of the Jewish leaders to do so. We are told, *"Saul, still breathing threats and murder against the disciples of the Lord, went to the high priest and asked letters from him to the synagogues of Damascus, so that if he found any who were of the Way, whether men or women, he might bring them bound to Jerusalem"* (Acts 9:1-2).

As he neared the outskirts of Damascus, he was suddenly dazed by a blinding flash of light. It knocked him to the ground and he heard a voice:

"Saul, Saul, why are you persecuting Me?" (Acts 9:4).

Saul wanted to know, *"Who are You?"*

The Lord answered, *"I am Jesus, whom you are persecuting"* (verse 5).

Astonished and trembling, Saul asked, *"Lord, what do you want me to do?"*

Jesus told him, *"Get up, go into the city and you will be told what to do."*

Those who were with him were confused. They could hear the sound, but they could not see anyone. Then, when Saul stood up, he found himself totally blind. Suddenly unable to see, his friends had to lead him into Damascus.

There was a follower of Jesus in the city named Ananias. In a vision, God instructed him where Saul was and, upon arriving at that house, Ananias told him, *"Saul, the Lord Jesus, who appeared to you on the road as you came, has sent me that you may receive your sight and be filled with the Holy Spirit"* (verse 17).

Immediately, Saul's sight was restored; he arose and was baptized.

On a Mission

Saul wasted no time before he started preaching the Gospel in the synagogues. As a devout Jew, he knew the Scriptures well and proclaimed the Messiah who had transformed his life.

In those days, it wasn't uncommon for men to have dual names. The Bible refers to *"Saul, who is also called, Paul, filled with the Holy Spirit"* (Acts 13:9). From that point on, Scripture only calls him Paul.

When the church at Antioch wanted to send out missionaries, they chose Paul and Barnabas. In turn, the two men went to Cyprus and Turkey—not only preaching to the Jews, but also to the Gentiles (Acts 13).

His second journey was with Silas, where they stayed in Corinth for about a year.

The third was three years of productive ministry in Ephesus (Acts 20). That mission ended in Jerusalem, after which Paul spent most of his next ten years in various prisons. Despite being confined, he was never alone, for God's power was with him!

It was as if Paul knew the turmoil he faced and how *"the Holy Spirit testifies in every city, saying that chains and tribulations await me"* (Acts 20:23).

The persecutions didn't seem to faze him. As he wrote, *"None of these things move me; nor do I count my life dear to myself, so that I may finish my race with joy, and the ministry which I received from the Lord Jesus, to testify to the gospel of the grace of God"* (verse 24).

Paul's life reads like a thrilling fiction novel, but that does not alter the fact that it is all true! He was kidnapped (Acts 21:27), beaten (verses 30-31), arrested (verse 33), accused in lawsuits (verse 34), threatened (Acts 22:22), ridiculed (Acts 26:24), shipwrecked (Acts 27:41), and bitten by a viper (Acts 28:3).

An Anointing for All

The secret of Paul's effective ministry was that he learned and accepted the purpose of suffering for Christ. He wrote that God *"comforts us in all our tribulation, that we may be able to comfort those who are in any trouble"* (2 Corinthians 1:4).

Of the 27 books of the New Testament, 13 are attributed to Paul—including the four he wrote from prison ... Ephesians, Philippians, Colossians, and Philemon.

The apostle preached that God's anointing was for all Christians, not just for the select few we read about in the Old Testament. To the believers at Corinth he wrote that it is God *"who establishes us with you in Christ and has anointed us ... [and] has given us the Spirit in our hearts as a guarantee"* (2 Corinthians 1:21).

This incredible blessing extends to you and me!

chapter 32

God's Presence and Power on
TIMOTHY

On Paul the apostle's first missionary journey, he preached in Lystra (Acts 14)—the home town of a young man named Timothy. Evidently, he was one of the converts, because when Paul went back to Lystra with Silas, *"Behold, a certain disciple was there, named Timothy"* (Acts 16:1).

Paul ordained Timothy into the ministry and refers to it when he writes, *"Do not neglect the gift that is in you, which was given to you by prophecy with the laying on of the hands of the eldership"* (1 Timothy 4:14). Obviously, Paul took part in the ordination, since he later mentions, *"I remind you to stir up the gift of God which is in you through the laying on of my hands"* (2 Timothy 1:6).

During the years that followed, Timothy became Paul's constant companion and co-worker in ministry. He was still a young man when he joined Paul, but he had already distinguished himself as a faithful follower of Christ, filled with the Holy Spirit, and a role model for other believers.

GENUINE FAITH

Timothy served as Paul's representative to several churches. He notified the congregation at Corinth, *"I have sent Timothy to you, who is my beloved and faithful son in the Lord, who will remind you of my ways in Christ, as I teach everywhere in every church"* (1 Corinthians 4:17). And to the believers at Philippi, *"I trust in the Lord Jesus to send Timothy to you shortly"* (Philippians 2:18).

However, Timothy became the pastor at Ephesus in his own right (1 Timothy 1:3).

There are two letters in the New Testament from Paul bearing Timothy's name. In one of Paul's letters, he told Timothy, *"I call to remembrance the genuine faith that is in you, which dwelt first in your grandmother Lois and your mother Eunice, and I am persuaded is in you also"* (2 Timothy 1:5).

The words used by Paul to counsel Timothy in his epistles hold timeless wisdom that is still available to each of us today:

You've learned the word of faith—now pass it on (1 Timothy 4:6).

Don't let anyone put you down because of your youth (verse 12).

Run hard and fast in the faith (1 Timothy 6:11).

Guard the spiritual treasure you have been entrusted with (verse 20).

You can only keep going by the power of God (2 Timothy 1:8).

What you have has been placed in your custody by the Holy Spirit (verse 14).

Every word of Scripture is God-breathed
(2 Timothy 3:16).

A Crown of Righteousness

As Paul's days were becoming shorter, the one person he wanted by his side was Timothy.

In the apostle's final letter, he wrote, *"The time of my departure is at hand. I have fought the good fight, I have finished the race, I have kept the faith. Finally, there is laid up for me the crown of righteousness, which the Lord, the righteous Judge, will give to me on that Day, and not to me only but also to all who have loved His appearing"* (1 Timothy 4:6-8).

Then Paul pleaded, *"Be diligent to come to me quickly … Do your utmost to come before winter … The Lord Jesus Christ be with your spirit. Grace be with you. Amen"* (verses 9, 21-22).

These were the last words penned by Paul. They echo a timeless reminder of the call upon every Christ follower to finish well.

chapter 33

God's Presence and Power on
SMITH WIGGLESWORTH

In the early 1900s, thousands flocked to a huge auditorium in Washington, D.C. to hear the preaching of a man from England who was known as "The apostle of faith." His name was Smith Wigglesworth.

During that meeting a young girl entered the building on crutches, helped by two other people. The girl's legs dangled beneath her because she had no muscular ability.

When Wigglesworth called for those who needed prayer to walk to the front, she struggled to move. He saw her difficulty and called out,

"Stay right where you are. You are going to be a different girl when you leave this place."

Wigglesworth asked about her condition and found out that she had never walked a day in her life. He laid his hands on her and commanded, "In the name of Jesus, walk."

TO THE AMAZEMENT OF EVERYONE PRESENT, SHE DROPPED HER CRUTCHES AND TOOK HER FIRST STEPS!

The Plumber and the Power

Smith Wigglesworth, born in 1859, was raised in an extremely poor family. His dad was a common laborer, and at the age of six, young Smith was pulling turnips to help with the family income.

Even as a boy, he had a hunger in his heart to know God. This led him to pray in the fields as he worked. Later, at a Wesleyan church meeting, he gave his life to Christ.

While still a teen, the Salvation Army in his area was experiencing an unusual outpouring of God in their services. He describes meetings where "many would be prostrate under the power of the Spirit, sometimes for as long as twenty-four hours."

Wigglesworth longed to see that anointing active in his own life. At 18, he became a plumber, but he spent every spare moment telling people about the Lord.

A real turning point was when he attended a "divine healing service" in the city of Leeds. He heard the message, *"They will lay hands on the sick, and they will recover"* (Mark 16:18).

At the time, Wigglesworth was suffering with hemorrhoids, so he anointed himself with oil according to James 5:14, and the condition never returned.

After a personal Pentecostal experience, he began to preach with a boldness that shook believers, churches, and cities. He was convinced that God didn't intend for believers to suffer. As a result, he approached praying for the sick as a battle between God and satan. It was clear that he lived expectant for God to be victorious over the darkness.

Wigglesworth said, "I have no word for rheumatism only 'demon possessed.' Rheumatism, cancers, tumors, lumbago, neuralgia, all these things I give only one name, the power of the devil working in humanity. When I see consumption, I see demon working power there. All these things can be removed."

In Europe, Asia, and America, crowds of up to 20,000 attended his meetings. He would pray unashamedly for the blind to see, the deaf to hear, and the lame to walk.

It is recorded that while he and a friend were praying for a woman in a hospital, she suddenly died. Wigglesworth literally took her out of the bed, stood her against the wall, and shouted, "In the name of Jesus I rebuke this death." Instantly, her whole body began to tremble. So he said, "In the name of Jesus, walk"—and she did!

In large gatherings where he couldn't pray for people personally, he asked everyone who needed healing to lay hands on themselves as he fervently called on God.

HUNDREDS EXPERIENCED A MIRACLE OF HEALING AT ONE TIME.

Smith Wigglesworth left a legacy of introducing many to God's incredible power!

This minister consistently reminded those who attended his gatherings to look to Jesus as the Anointed One.

If he was still with us today, I believe he would remind each person that this power of the Holy Spirit, which includes the anointing to release healing, belongs to every devoted follower of Christ, not just to the leaders and ministers of our day.

chapter 34

God's Presence and Power on
AIMEE SEMPLE MCPHERSON

Centuries ago, the prophet Joel wrote, *"And it shall come to pass ... says God, that I will pour out My Spirit on all flesh; your sons and your daughters shall prophesy"* (Joel 2:28).

Without question, one of those anointed "daughters" was Aimee Semple McPherson.

Born and raised in Ontario, Canada, at the age of 17 she attended a revival service conducted by Pentecostal evangelist Robert Semple. She had a born-again experience and received the baptism of the Holy Spirit. From that day forward, Aimee was a transformed person!

That revival also changed her romantically, and in 1908, just before her 18th birthday, she and the evangelist were married. Soon they felt the tug of God on their lives to be missionaries in China.

Two years later, after arriving in Hong Kong, they both contracted malaria, and within three months, Robert died. This tragedy left Aimee widowed and penniless as she prepared to give birth to their first child. When the baby, a daughter named Roberta Star Semple, was just one month old, Aimee had no other choice but to return to the United States as a single mom.

Aimee's mother had moved to New York City, and that's where she headed. There she helped her mom raise funds for the Salvation Army. Soon after, she met a Christian businessman, Harold McPherson. They fell in love, were married, and had a son whom they named Rolf.

Now the mother of two children, she put off her call to preach and became a homemaker. Sadly, Aimee's health declined, and after two major surgeries, she lay near death in a hospital bed. It was there the Lord asked her, "Now will you go?"

Aimee answered, "Yes" and was almost immediately healed. She never questioned the Lord's call to ministry again.

Harold and Aimee started holding tent revivals where many were saved and healed. But living in near poverty made things almost impossible. Eventually, Harold decided this wasn't the life he wanted, and the two separated.

"Sister Aimee," as she was called, continued to evangelize on her own, and before long even the largest tents could not hold the crowds. At auditoriums, people stood in line for hours to get a seat.

IN SAN DIEGO THEY HAD TO CALL IN THE NATIONAL GUARD TO HELP CONTROL A CROWD OF MORE THAN 30,000!

She preached salvation and healing to the rich and poor. She fearlessly worked to tear down ethnic barriers and segregation everywhere she went. She was a true pioneer whose legacy still calls us to a life of complete devotion.

Angelus Temple

Tired of having no permanent place to call home and raise a family, she rejoiced when the Lord told her to go to Los Angeles, where He would build her a house. Actually, He built two houses—one for her and her family, and one for the people.

Many caught the vision of a giant auditorium to be called Angelus Temple. In 1923, when she was 32 years old, the 5,300-seat building was dedicated. The ministry facility was filled to capacity in every service.

Her illustrated sermons on Sunday nights were the talk of the town. Hundreds of newspapers printed her sermons, and after launching a radio station with a powerful signal, she became one of the best-known voices in America. She also founded the Foursquare denomination that is thriving to this day.

Because of her fame, Aimee was kidnapped in 1926 and held for ransom. When released, her ministry grew even larger. The media, however, had a field day with rumors of her personal life, which persisted until she died in 1944.

Today, there are untold thousands, if not millions, who are in God's kingdom because of this dedicated servant of the Lord.

God's heart is to anoint His daughters from every nation and every walk of life. Imagine how the world would be transformed if every girl and woman began believing that she had been placed on earth to fulfill a unique Kingdom assignment. If you are a woman, ask God to increase your vision for your own life. If you are a man, ask God to reveal how you can encourage and awaken the Kingdom treasure hidden inside the hearts of the women you interact with daily.

chapter 35

God's Presence and Power on
KATHRYN KUHLMAN

I can hear her now. After finding Kathryn Kuhlman's program on my radio dial, her first words were always the same: "Hello there! And have you been waiting for me? It's so nice of you. I just knew you'd be there."

From her home town of Pittsburgh, Pennsylvania, this mighty woman of God carried an anointing that no one could doubt. It literally radiated from her presence as she preached in her flowing white dresses and saw miracle after miracle.

Born in Concordia, Missouri in 1907, Kathryn was saved at the age of 14 in a small Methodist church. Her older sister, Myrtle, had married a traveling evangelist, Everett B. Parrott, and Kathryn joined them during the summer months. She loved the ministry so much that her parents eventually let her stay with them, which she did for the next five years.

In Boise, Idaho, Everett had to miss a meeting, and the two sisters filled in. Kathryn captured the attention of the audience so much that the pastor told Kathryn, "You need to start preaching." She did, and her first sermon was in a rundown pool hall.

The team decided to move to Pueblo, Colorado, where a revival broke out and they held services for six months in an abandoned Montgomery Ward warehouse. In 1935, they moved to Denver. By then, God's anointing rested so heavily on Kathryn that she was doing most of the preaching. They called the church Denver Revival Tabernacle as it grew to over 2,000 members.

"I Believe in Miracles"

After marrying an evangelist, Burroughs Waltrip, the two began a ministry in Mason City, Iowa, where they conducted revivals across the country. The marriage, however, seemed doomed from the start, and they divorced in 1947.

Now on her own, she accepted an invitation to hold a revival in Franklin, Pennsylvania. She was so well received that she decided to remain in the area. This led her to start a radio broadcast that reached the city of Pittsburgh.

In her meetings, amazing miracles began to take place. A woman was healed of a tumor, a man testified that his vision was restored, and people were rejoicing.

In 1948 Kuhlman held a series of meetings at Carnegie Hall in Pittsburgh and moved to the city permanently in 1950. Her radio program was heard nationally and her weekly telecast, I Believe in Miracles, was aired coast to coast in the 1960s and '70s.

Obviously, the world was paying attention to this dynamic woman preacher, and even popular culture recognized her. She appeared on The Tonight Show with Johnny Carson in 1974, and was mentioned on more than one occasion on the Mary Tyler Moore Show, as well as The Carol Burnett Show.

A Faith Healer?

Wherever she spoke, it was as if Heaven itself descended to Earth. For several years, she held Tuesday services at the First Presbyterian Church in Pittsburgh. Busloads traveled from across the nation and it was almost impossible to find a seat in the sanctuary. While Kathryn was the mouthpiece, it was the Lord who was speaking through His servant. The presence of Almighty God was so strong in those meetings that many in the congregation literally felt the wind of the Spirit blowing on them.

In addition to this, she held regular services

at the Shrine Auditorium in Los Angeles. Those she prayed for would be hit and overcome with God's power, falling to the floor, literally "slain in the Spirit."

SHE REFUSED TO CALL
HERSELF A "FAITH HEALER,"
ALWAYS POINTING PEOPLE
TO JESUS AS THE ONE
WHO DOES THE HEALING.

Kathryn Kuhlman passed from this life in 1976 following open heart surgery. I know she received a glorious welcome in Heaven after leading so many into the presence of the Lord.

Kathryn's ministry began in a pool hall, leaving a reminder that God wants to minister through each of us in ordinary places. Be on the lookout for opportunities to release His light and love into your home, your community, your workplaces, and beyond. God desires for every life to leave a lasting legacy of faith.

chapter 36

God's Presence and Power on
ORAL ROBERTS

For five months, a 17-year-old boy in Ada, Oklahoma, was bedridden with tuberculosis. His weight had plummeted to 120 pounds and, for his height, he was practically a skeleton. His name was Oral.

His parents were strong Christians and faithfully prayed for him every day. They didn't understand why God did not heal their son, especially since, while his mother was pregnant, she committed him to God's service.

The Roberts family was extremely poor, and when Oral was 16, he moved away from home, dreaming of a better life. At the same time, he turned his back on God and began living a wild life; that's when his health collapsed.

The Lord spoke to Oral's older sister Jewel and let her know that her brother was going to be healed. About the same time, Oral gave his life to Christ.

A traveling healing evangelist, George Moncey, came to Ada and pitched a tent. Oral's brother decided to bring him to one of the meetings.

ON THE WAY TO THE TENT,
GOD CLEARLY SPOKE
TO ORAL, SAYING,
"SON, I AM GOING
TO HEAL YOU AND
YOU ARE TO TAKE
MY HEALING POWER
TO YOUR GENERATION."

In the meeting, Oral was too weak to walk to the front for prayer so he waited for the evangelist to come to him. It was 11:00 at night before Moncey laid hands on him and anointed him with oil. The power of God washed over Oral and he was instantly healed. Not only did the tuberculosis disappear, but Oral, who suffered from a severe stuttering problem, discovered that was gone too!

Roberts was ordained by the Pentecostal Holiness church in 1936, and soon became an outstanding minister of the denomination. In the next few years he pastored four of their churches with his new bride, Evelyn.

HEALING WATERS

In 1947, the Lord strongly impressed Oral to get down on his knees and read the four Gospels and the book of Acts three times consecutively. This was when God began to reveal Jesus as the healer in a unique and powerful way. Immediately, Oral began to hold special healing meetings in his town and miracles began to multiply. When a deranged man tried to shoot him, the national media picked up the story and people were flocking to his meetings as never before.

On faith, he resigned as pastor and purchased a tent that seated 2,000. Soon, it wasn't big enough to hold the crowds, so he found one that held 12,500 and launched the Oral Roberts Evangelistic Association.

Within months, his Healing Waters magazine was being published, and films of his crusades became a weekly television program that my family watched every week. Later in this book, you will read how it played a part in my own healing.

The monthly magazine was renamed Abundant Life in 1956, and eventually reached a circulation of over one million. His monthly column appeared in over 600 newspapers, and by 1980, more than 15 million of his 88 books had sold.

Many observers credit Oral Roberts with bringing the Pentecostal message and the charismatic movement into the mainstream of religion in the United States and abroad.

HE WAS HONORED
AND RESPECTED
AS A MAN OF INTEGRITY
AND INVITED TO SPEAK AT
MAJOR INTERDENOMINATIONAL
EVENTS WORLDWIDE.

Billy Graham was the featured speaker at the dedication of Oral Roberts University.

After a life of faithful service, Roberts retired in 1993 and went to be with his heavenly Father in 2009 at the advanced age of 91.

The Lord called a young boy from Oklahoma who readily answered, and the world was touched by God's power. His life of devotion still reminds believers to never lose sight of how the Lord wants to touch the world through us. Take the challenge which ignited Oral's legacy of faith. Get alone and dive deep into the four Gospels and the book of Acts. Envision your life being added to those who took the Good News to the corners of the globe!

chapter 37

God's Presence *and* Power *on*
ME

At the age of ten, I was in a Birmingham, Alabama, hospital room, suffering from hepatitis C with yellow jaundice. It had infected my liver, which was dangerously swollen and threatening to burst. Doctors were breaking the bad news to my family, "His liver is destroyed, and he will probably only live for five to eight more days at the most."

On a Sunday morning, at about 9:00 a.m., my mother, Josephine, and my aunt turned on the television in the hospital room and were watching Oral Roberts's program, "The Healing Hour."

At one point in the telecast, Roberts looked into the camera and said, "I am going to ask you to touch the television if you possibly can. If not, reach out your hand toward the screen as a point of contact as I pray for your healing."

Well, my mother, doing as he asked, reached over and touched the television screen with one hand while her other hand rested on my stomach. She then uttered these words: "God heal my boy and I will give him to You."

Instantly—not in a minute, not next week or next month—the power of God entered the room.

I can still see it in my mind's eye. It was like light illuminating a mist, and standing in the middle of the brightness was Jesus. The power was so tangible that it literally knocked my mother and aunt to the floor.

The doctors and assistants at the nursing station saw the light reflecting from my room and ran down the hall to see what was happening. The power of God was so tangible and intense that an orderly rushed in with a fire extinguisher! They didn't know what to think when they saw my mother and aunt lying on the floor as if they had been knocked out cold.

God's power showed up that day to such an extent that I was completely healed. When the doctors called for tests that afternoon, they were speechless to find that I had absolutely no signs of disease in my body. There was not even a residue of hepatitis C in my blood.

I was a healthy young man—totally healed!

THE MANIFESTATION

It is one thing to read about the power and presence of God in the lives of men and women in Bible days, and the miracles the Lord is still performing today, but God longs to use you and me to impact the lives of others.

Many years after the Lord touched me in that hospital room, I began to teach and preach on the subject of healing. I was not conscious of any special gift or manifestation, but as I laid hands on the sick and asked God to heal them—He did!

I have been praying for people in the name of Jesus ever since.

In the Panama Canal Zone, I shared my testimony and asked men, women, and children to walk forward for prayer. The first woman told me through the interpreter that she had a bleeding ulcer. I anointed her with oil and prayed, then went on to the next person.

Suddenly, I turned around and saw the first woman vomit up the ulcer on the floor. She was totally healed by the power of God. I had never witnessed anything like that before in my life.

Today, after many years of ministry, I have seen countless miracles—crossed eyes straightened, deaf ears unstopped, arthritic hands opened, and so much more.

Our God is the Great Physician not only of our failing bodies, but also our minds and spirits!

chapter 38

God's Presence and Power on
YOU!

Everything up to this point is a prologue. You have seen the presence and power of God poured out on the Old and New Testament saints, on Spirit-filled men and women, including me. But what about you?

What's the point of knowing about divine power, but never experiencing it personally? What good is it to read of the presence and anointing of the Spirit, if it has never touched your life?

The omnipotent God is much more than speaking the world into existence; it affects you. The prayer of the Apostle Paul needs to also be yours: *"... that I may know Him and the power of His resurrection"* (Philippians 3:10).

Salvation is instantaneous, but the fullness of God develops over a lifetime. As Paul continues, *"Not that I have already attained, or am already perfected; but I press on, that I may lay hold of that for which Christ Jesus has also laid hold of me"* (verse 12).

The Lord wants you to grasp the magnitude of His mighty power that saved you from the clutches of satan, so that you can represent Christ to a dying world.

Life-Giving Power and Presence

Instead of standing in the shadows, being in awe of the Spirit of God that rested on Jesus, claim it for yourself. *"If the Spirit of Him who raised Jesus from the dead dwells in you, He who raised Christ from the dead will also give life to your mortal bodies through His Spirit who dwells in you"* (Romans 11:11).

Those who profess to know Jesus need to ask themselves, "Do I really have a new life in Christ? If I was dead in my sins and am now alive through His resurrection power, why isn't it being demonstrated daily?"

Regardless of your circumstances, even if you don't feel you have the stamina to face another day, God wants to energize your very soul and raise you up: *"He gives power to the weak, and to those who have no might He increases strength"* (Isaiah 40:29).

On our own we are weak, but He is strong. This is why Paul wrote, *"We have this treasure in earthen vessels, that the excellence of the power may be of God and not of us"* (2 Corinthians 4:7).

The reason Jesus promised to send God's Spirit to earth was to give us the ability and authority to evangelize: *"But you shall receive power when the Holy Spirit has come upon you; and you shall be witnesses to Me in Jerusalem, and in all Judea and Samaria, and to the end of the earth"* (Acts 1:8).

I have conducted hundreds of services in many parts of the world, and one thing I have learned. It's only when the presence of God shows up that lives are transformed, sick bodies are healed, and people receive deliverance.

I've discovered that the Lord does not share His power randomly. He wants us to *"Seek first the kingdom of God and His righteousness, and all these things shall be added unto you"* (Matthew 6:33). There is a divine order for those who long to tap into God's limitless power and presence.

Don't wait another minute to pray for the anointing—and get ready for a spiritual earthquake!

The Lord is closer than we think: *"He is not far from each one of us; for in Him we live and move and have our being"* (Acts 17:27-28).

Rejoice with the psalmist: *"In Your presence there is fullness of joy, at Your right hand are pleasures forevermore"* (Psalm 16:11).

God's power and plans are for YOU ... and they are found only In His Presence!

FOR BOOKS AND MEDIA RESOURCES
OR TO SCHEDULE THE AUTHOR FOR
MINISTRY AND SPEAKING ENGAGEMENTS,
INCLUDING MEDIA INTERVIEWS,
CONTACT:

Tommy Combs
Healing Word
Living Word Ministries

ADDRESS: P. O. Box 1000, Dora, AL 35062
PHONE: 866-391-WORD (9673)
EMAIL: tommy.livingwordbooks@gmail.com
WEBSITE: www.evangelisttommycombs.org